Lost Lake

Folk Opera

Winter 2018-2019   Volume 5 Number 2

In Memoriam

Scott Dixon
Pixie Youngdahl
Donna Halvorson
Dean Harrington

SHIPWRECKT BOOKS PUBLISHING COMPANY L.L.C.
Rocket Science Press
Lost Lake Folk Art

Up On Big Rock Poetry Series
Lost Lake Folk Opera

Lost Lake Folk Opera is a Shipwreckt Books imprint
published annually.
Letters to the editor are always welcome.
Submissions welcome online at
www.shipwrecktbooks.press

309 W. Stevens Ave.	Rushford, Minnesota, 55971
507 458 8190	contact@shipwrecktbooks.com
Managing Editor	Tom Driscoll
Publisher	Beth Stanford

www.shipwrecktbooks.com

WWW.SHIPWRECKTBOOKS.COM

Cover and all interior photos by Shipwreckt Books unless otherwise indicated.

In this issue

Check out our new website at www.shipwrecktbooks.press

Scott Lowery
Six Poems

The Rabbit

Among the dry brush, it's only
his sameness that stands out.
All neutrals, brown on brown,
fully absent. He ambles, stops,
drops from sight—nope,
still there. So much backdrop!
Someone's smiling—me or the rabbit?

Painting the Cow
Cow 3 of 9, oil painting by Brianna Berghuis

The cow has no issue with being painted.
She lifts her massive muzzle to you,
    black as a tire, wet as a sponge.
Her fermented breath condenses,
    snot dotted with bits of straw.

You can use raw milk across her forehead.
Mix in egg yolk for that unexpected
    yellow at her jaw line:
a smear of morning sun.

The cow is not self-conscious, wearing
    her dapper crust of dung,
giving you a gold-brown edge to set
    against the cold white sky.

If she's discontented, the cow
keeps it to herself for now,
    though she could step on you
with the weight of a small truck.

Her big ears flap like soft slippers,
    ready to hear your thoughts.
Light plays on the pool
    of a watchful, inky eye.

If you're quick
you can stick the sharp legs
    of your easel into the muck
and get to work.

Looking for a Horse Poem after an Eye Exam
for Ken McCullough

Let's start with the chemical sting of the eyedrops,
the chemical tears they evoke soaking in, if that's what they do,
the chemical pin-prick of fear and wonder released in my blood, racing
to bang on the door of my brain with the news that soon,
my pupils will lose all their common sense,
will relax wide open to every random photon bouncing around in the world,
not yet but soon, maybe when the ophthalmologist returns to check on my
    dilated progress,
here in my Star Command chair, crying comfortably into my Kleenex.

Not yet but soon—this reminds me of when I'd lose what common sense I had,
a teenage seeker after chemical enhancement of the given world
with all its dull complicity, its murderous suits and ties.
I'd drop a tab and wait like this, to feel an accelerant current start to pull me
    downstream.
A poem can do that too, or the chemical seed of a poem.
For instance, the poet who hosts our monthly open mic has suggested a poem on
    horses,
an animal inexplicably absent from all the years of my writing,
a decades-long drought of horse poems, trailing back into the dust.
My poet friend is a longtime keeper of horses, can read a horse like a four-legged
    book of Complete Horse Poems,
understands each electric skin quiver, each gum-flap and muzzle nudge.

All I can remember about horses is their inky brown eyes:
expressive or opaque, serene or startled, curious or disinterested.

In horses' eyes, I have seen my own big-nosed reflection, and over my
    shoulder the rest of the curving world.
As the exam resumes, as the doc beams his tiny lantern into each red cave and says they're fine,
I am thinking of a horse's head, with its two huge eyes, imploring, yet not turning
    into a poem,
and even less so out in the sun-lit parking lot,
where I squint through banged-up clip-ons into a barrage of too much light, too
    much world.

Before I can go home and pull the blinds, I have errands to run,
so I crawl my car impeccably through translucent intersections,
past loud, shimmering objects moving with deadly intent,
to arrive at Fleet Farm, and another parking lot
    where the faucet of the world's light won't turn off.
They sell chemicals here to soften limestone-laden household water,
a secular miracle heretofore as unremarked as horses in my poems.
Among the aisles, shades still on, I can barely see one thing after another,
    until I'm brought to a sudden stop—
towering above me, a life-sized fiberglass horse, shiny as a toy,
stands expressionless and stoic atop a stack of steel shelves.
Around his neck, an employee nametag reads "Hello, my name is Sea Biscuit."
You think I'm making this up? The world is making this up.

Isn't common sense called horse sense? What's he doing up there?
Unfiltered questions start pouring into my bloodstream,
and all the building supplies of a serviceable poem are suddenly at hand, but I'm
    blocking the aisle.
These folks have their own lists, their own miracles.
Even the plastic dairy cow four aisles over seems disinterested,
gazing off the other way, toward the spring crop of fishing lures and herbicide
    and semi-automatic rifles.

Let me step out of the flow here.
Common sense would say this is not really a horse poem, or a miracle, or a
    chemistry experiment, and yet
it is oxygenated, it leads to an everyday-yet-unexplainable vision,
it contains at least one horse—
and common sense never wrote a poem.
So let us praise God, or science, or the devil mustangs of chance,
praise Customer Service and the marketing miracles of the digitally-gifted—
in other words, praise for the visible, unstoppable world:
praise for the lens, praise for the light,
praise for words that can run on their own four legs.

Reset / Morning After

"The sun will rise in the morning…" Barack Obama

Yes, and blaze on the glass—
don't forget: a long look
can blind you.

The birds will pour their hearts
into something once
called singing,

while the last fluttering flags,
still golden on the maple,
must come down.

What does the wind want,
but to tear the skin off
the fallow fields?

No matter how sad they look,
it won't pay to keep them—
let the cows go.

Plow the dreamer's books into
the ditch. Get the gas can.
Stand and watch.

Inaugural Ghazal

If only this throbbing tooth would never grind or grate again!
I'll vote for ibuprofen: it'll make my mouth feel great again.

The chickadee, wholly absorbed in each moment's hull and seed—
No interest in the hard-shelled nut of being great again.

Over the whine of his ATV, a neighbor boy rides tall in the saddle.
He fills his tank for a ten-dollar bill and gasoline smells great again.

The sanctity of the locker room's restored at last, thank you Lord.
PC's been purged—it's great to all be white and straight again.

Grandpa taught me how to rhyme on his bony, sing-song knee.
Catch a nigger by the toe: he thought it sounded great back then.

The young drone pilot, poised all night above his glowing screen.
Nothing like rubble and blood to make a country great again.

Pulled from line, a family stands with widened, dark-brown eyes.
Isn't it great to breeze right through, relieved *you* won't be late again?

Big Daddy Warbucks, back in the house, dripping glitz and bling.
He's all like *Let the good times roll*, now that the NASDAQ's great again.

Go find the Comeback King, old Bonaparte in his iron cell.
Ask him how that went—does he still desire to be great again?

Five hundred sovereign treaties, each one so carefully broken.
Sitting Bull has the talking stick, before you claim to be great again.

So let's gather now, with songs in praise of Justice's beautiful body.
We'll finger-sift her ashes, and hammer on God's gate again.

And you, Lowery—knocked flat by our national freight again?
It's cold out here and the moon is thin, but it will be great again.

Norma Rae as a Honey Bee

Since daylight, she's been knocking on doors
in high-rise rows of corn where no one's home.
Next, she'll follow a nitrate trail downhill
to scrappy pastures by the silted creek,
blue-collar lots of coneflower and butterfly weed
as rare as decent housing and a union wage:

back-roads pushed further back each year,
cows thinned out by mass incarceration.
Along the highway, she hovers to watch a guy
in Day-Glo vest and Carhartt bibs mowing ditch hay,
the cardboard No Spray sign buried in his wake.
Gentlemen: your average working bee is not stupid.
She just gets tired.
    That bit's a voice-over—
no swarm of New York lawyers to call in—
so she re-straightens her tiny shoulders
and moves on, ready to dodge cars along parkways,
sail the edges of alleys, wherever she can pick up
that river of vibration that still calls itself a Sisterhood.
Last week, she had her Oscar-winning moment,
imploring pollinators and poisoners alike
with those honeyed, fractal eyes.
When the cops hauled her off in their net,
the whole hive hit the bricks and nearly
lost their way home. Now they wait in the dark,
hoping against the odds for a new Queen,
crossing their multiple, yellow-caked legs,
    while Norma quietly made bail and got back to work,
One Big Union embroidered on her DNA.
She's a free-range blossom, a scrupled sting
in that song she hums: Which side *are* you on?
Here she comes now, as the credits start to roll,
overloaded with leaflets, zig-zagging low over asphalt
and thistle, manure lagoons and drainage tile,
our stitcher of invisible thread,
our busy beacon, too small to fail.

Maria L. Souza Hogan
Samba of Survival—Scrounging in the Slums of Brazil

When I was almost seven, Father got sick with a terrible pain that would not go away. At first, Mother believed it was not serious, and that it would soon be cured using the herbal teas and concoctions from plants in our back yard, like many other maladies that she was used to diagnosing and treating. This one, however, was different. The pain got worse, not better. My sister Gaia and elder brothers Célio and Carlos—nicknamed Tatai—took turns walking the long road to the town pharmacy to ask Orlando Lima, the pharmacist and a son of Aunt Zibina's daughter, Iaiá, to please come and help.

Soon after Father died, Mother began pacing the dirt floor on one side of our house where a white jasmine bush in constant bloom emanated a soothing aroma. She carried Wilson, our 6-month old baby brother, in her arms, and wondered where our next meal would come from. At the time, my brothers and sisters decided to help bring in some food or money any way that they could.

Club of Stars will be released in the fall of 2019.

Ua, the eldest at nineteen, barely four feet tall with light skin, dark hair and eyes, took a job at the local movie theater after one of our cousin's boyfriend did the cousin the evil deed—"fez o mal a ela," and she was forced to leave her job. She "was lost"—"se perdeu." After a boy had deflowered a girl in town—"deflorou a moca"—in most cases, the girl was forced to leave her parents' home—"sair de casa." These popular expressions indicated a girl's loss of her virginity, a way of saying that a boy had gotten her pregnant. A girl's virginity was sacred, and it had to be preserved until marriage. If it was lost, everyone would ostracize her, including her family. She would lose a job—if she had one—her humanity, and the respect of the community. Parents would usually send their daughters to stay with a distant relative or the girl had to stay indoors, not leaving the parents' home for the duration of the pregnancy. I often heard the elders say that these girls could never lead a normal life again.

There were girls I remember seeing in the neighborhood who had no distant relatives to take them in. They had no means of leaving home or raising the child. The grandparents assumed responsibility for raising the baby, and the girls stayed prisoners in their parents' home and were never again accepted in society. However, after our cousin had her child, as if by miracle, she got married to a former boyfriend and started a family. But after a few years, her husband left her for a young girl whom she raised and lived in the family's home, helping with the children and the chores.

Ua would take all of the money she earned at her new job and at a second one she had at the *Cartorio Eleitoral*—where she recorded the townspeople's voting records and registration by hand—to the market on Saturday to buy food. In addition, the sewing classes Ua had taken in better days on Flowers Street were put into practice to supplement her earnings at her two other jobs. Soon, the front window of our rundown house gained color with the display of the undergarments my sister and mother sewed on the new Singer that Father had bought before his illness. They hung the clothes on a rope across the top frame. Neighbors and passersby would stop and take notice.

Surrounded by colorful panties and brassieres on the window sill was fresh yellow corn meal couscous, topped with white grated coconut. Mother made and sliced it into triangular portions to sell to the workers who walked by our house in the early morning on their way to Suerdieck, the town's tobacco factory. The smell of the sweet corn filled the air. We couldn't eat the couscous because we knew that Mother sold it so that we could buy beans and farina, and maybe a small piece of dry meat to cook with the beans. The beans and farina would fill our stomachs more and make us less hungry. Later, Mother also sold couscous to buy some of my schoolbooks. By midmorning, Mother's couscous was usually gone.

To make her couscous, Mother would soak the corn overnight, drain the water early in the morning and pound the soft kernels in the large, tall, and thick black wood mortar with a heavy black pestle kept in the kitchen. Ua, Gaia, and other female neighbors would help Mother pound the corn. Two women would face each other and the wood mortar, stretch their arms way up, holding the heavy pestle with both hands to hit the kernels in a rhythmic and naturally coordinated up-and-down movement. One pestle would reach the bottom of the mortar in full force—pooh—while the other would stand up in the air; one woman's body would bend over the mortar while the other would stretch way back. They would perform this ballet for a while to the deep sound the pestle made when it thumped the mortar back and forth, pooh … pooh … pooh…. The neighbors also would pound coffee beans for hours this way, never touching each other's pestle and sometimes singing a popular jingle to the rhythm of the coordinated pounding:

I am pounding coffee. Vou pilar café.
I am pounding coffee. Vou pilar café.
Pound, pound my little sweetheart Pila, pila meu benzinho
That daddy does not want you to. Que papai não quer.

I never took my eyes away from the beloved women the whole time they ground corn or coffee in the backyard by our kitchen. Their rhythm, grace, and agility enchanted me. I can still see their body movement and hear the deep sound of the pestle hitting the mortar.

Gaia sewed mattresses and shirts for Vinicius, the owner of a store, from Monday to Friday and took the money that she earned to the market on Saturdays. I would walk with Gaia to the store early Monday to get a big bundle of fabric for the cutting and sewing and would stroll back late Friday with the sewn shirts and mattresses bundled up on our heads. On Saturday, I happily would march with Gaia, the money, and our dark vine basket to the market.

Gaia, seventeen when Father died, tall, slender, agile with cinnamon skin, very dark hair and eyes, and a luminous smile, displayed a very practical approach to things and immediately thought of a new way to put food in our dark clay pan on the wood burning stove when we were hungry and there was no food in the house. In the backyard, a parade of chickens, pigs, and roosters would appear and disappear at random as they fed on earthworms, insects, and bits and pieces of whatever food that they found dispersed throughout the area. It was the neighbor's livestock. Gaia devised a plan to trap the clucking chickens in our kitchen by setting a white trail of farina or bits of earthworm. The animals would follow the trail and end up corralled in a small space in the kitchen where we waited for them.

Gaia would prepare for the event by sharpening a kitchen knife on our black stone, rubbing the knife back and forth and dropping water on the silver blade. She then set the knife by our clay bowl half filled with vinegar and put water to boil in the tall kerosene can on the stove. As soon as the chicken passed the doorframe, we carefully closed the wobbly door and chased the panicky animal into a corner. The chicken bounced back and forth against our kitchen walls and wood burning stove. The struggle did not last long, for the space was tight and the fast hands and empty stomachs were many.

Once Gaia had the chicken, she held it tightly down with her knee. She secured its head on a piece of wood, peeled off the fine feathers from its neck, tapped on it a few times, and slit the throat open with our shiny silver knife. She poured the warm blood into the clay bowl and mixed it with the vinegar so it would not coagulate. Sometimes when Gaia's knife missed the fatal vein, the stunned animal would stand up and circle the kitchen, dripping its red blood on the dirt floor and slamming its bloody head into the black walls. We would trap the disoriented animal in a hurry and give it back to our sister to finish the job with the razor-sharp knife and squeeze the remaining blood into the clay bowl. I helped Gaia immerse the chicken in a bath of cold water and then in the tall can of boiling water on the stove. We would gather to remove the feathers quickly and Gaia would cut the chicken into small pieces, making every part count: feet and guts, which we turned inside out to clean in the nearby pond and cut into small pieces to make a stew dish called *cabidela*. The chicken tripe was sometimes full of hookworms, but they did not bother Gaia. She flushed them out. Then my sister cooked the chicken in its blood.

We would put the wet feathers in a bucket and carry them to be buried in a carefully dug hole in the bushes very far from our house. We cooked the chicken with all the windows and doors closed so that the smell would not give us away. On those days we ate. When my sister attracted more than one chicken at a time, there was good reason for celebration: we ate more, and our feast and happiness were complete. And Gaia did not have to cut the pieces too small. There was enough for everyone in our family.

Our adventure with the neighbors' chickens went on for a while until our feast along with the frequent disappearance of the animals aroused suspicions. And then, at sundown, when the women walked home from the tobacco factory, and their chickens did not show up at the pen or the count of the flock was short, they would go looking for their animals. When they couldn't find them, they would stop right at our backyard by our kitchen door to ask if we had seen the chickens and describe the missing animal to us.

"Have you seen my chicken today?" they would ask.

"No. What chicken? We haven't," we would always answer.

"It was a young chicken with red stripes, and you must've seen it; we don't live too far from each other, and the chicken must've passed through your yard," they would insist.

"No. We haven't seen it," we replied.

"It was my golden hen that laid eggs like no other," some would lament.

"It was a plump white chicken," another desperate woman would explain.

"No, we haven't seen anything like it," was our persistent reply.

"Miserable bunch of liars and hungry thieves," they would yell angrily as they walked away.

We must not have been very convincing and soon the neighbors, one by one, started fencing up their yards and keeping their flocks in. One Friday afternoon, a neighbor named Maria de Mané Vito stood firmly by our kitchen door and demanded news about her black chicken that had disappeared that day. It was the chicken that she was planning on taking to be sacrificed to the voodoo gods at sundown. I had my heart and soul in my hands that evening but stood by the story of not having seen any chicken like that one. Maria left our house calling us names at the top of her lungs, and we soon became known as the miserable chicken thieves and liars in the neighborhood.

With the disappearance of the neighbors' chickens from our backyard, my siblings had to find another way to put food on the table. On Wednesday nights, looking for relief from the midweek hunger, one of my sisters, who, decades later, still feels ashamed of this sacrifice, would take me by the hand and walk across town to pay a visit to the local priest, Padre Pedro. The two would meet in the back of the town's tall whitewashed church, standing on a small hill in the center of town. The priest would appear in a long black robe after my sister's soft knock at the church's back door. He would greet us in a soft and pious voice, take my sister by the hand, and order me to stay quiet inside the church until my sister was finished and came for me.

"All right," I answered softly.

I did not know what the priest's finishing with my sister involved. I was eight, very afraid of the priest, fascinated, and scared by the images in the church. Padre Pedro wore a long black cape which brought to mind the stories of "The Man in the Black Cape" my siblings told us in the dark, on warm and quiet nights, sitting by the side of our house. A man in black was said to wander around town on pitch-dark nights—and there were testimonies of many people who swore to having seen him in our neighborhood, taking the women and children and scaring the men away. I had heard the stories many times over, sitting stiff and snuggled against my siblings in fear. The children and women the man in the black cape was said to kidnap were never to return, and nothing was ever known of their fate.

The voices of my siblings telling this story on pitch-dark nights played over and over in my head, as I entered the big white church in the shadows of candlelight. The angels with puffy round faces, lips, and hands holding a torch and the human sized statues of saints with sad faces and dressed in real clothes transported me to another world. I had never seen anything of the kind. I walked around in the dim light, and their eyes followed me everywhere I went. I could not hide from them. I sat on a pew in the back and waited.

My sister suddenly appeared, fixing her hair and straightening her red skirt with the palm of her hands. She walked to the back of the church and took me by the hand.

"Let's go home Leda," she whispered in a very low voice.

"Are we coming back to church again?" I asked.

"I don't know," she said. "And don't say anything to anyone about this," she warned me in a firm manner.

"Yes," I said with my head down. And we walked home without saying another word.

Much later in life, when I asked my sister to elaborate on our frequent visits to the town's priest on Wednesdays, she described the occasion as being very close to my recollection. But when I asked her what exactly she did in the back of the church with Padre Pedro, she laughed a bit for a while and replied that she was in the long line with the other poor people in town, waiting for the priest's charity to buy food for the family. Then my sister became serious and sad, her head down.

The nights my sister visited church we had some money for food the following morning. We would go to the stores in town with our basket because there was no open market on Thursdays. My sister did not have to worry about my revealing her visits to the priest. No one ever asked about it, though everyone knew that the priest gave my sister money on Wednesday nights. I was just happy the next day, hearing the firewood crackling, seeing the red flames under our black clay pot change from red to yellow engulfing the round black clay pot, and smelling the beans cooking. My sister knocked on the church's back door many more Wednesdays and met with the "Man in The Black Cape." I continued to follow her.

One of my father's sisters, Nininha, once decided to help our family and asked my sister Miriam, who was ten at the time, to help at her store on market day. Nininha lived on Church Street, across the wide street from her sister Didi. The store, which was up a hill just a short distance from her house, sold sugar, coffee, nuts, tobacco, cigars, leather and the kinds of dried goods that the vendors who came to town to sell their fresh produce took back with them. To Gaia, this was a very good opportunity to gather some money for our market day. She sewed a big pocket on the inside of Miriam's underpants and instructed my sister how to divert some of the cash from Aunt Nininha's register into her underwear pocket.

"You have to smile your natural way while doing it," Gaia said. "So, don't show any signs of being nervous."

"Fine. What do I do if people look at me? Miriam asked.

"Just pretend nothing happened, and you're just scratching yourself," replied Gaia.

Nininha's store was popular and prosperous. Since Miriam was eager to help us back home, it worked out well. My sister quickly learned to weigh coffee, sugar, tobacco, peanuts, and fill bottles of kerosene and palm oil to sell. She performed her new tasks efficiently. At the end of the day on Saturdays, she would arrive home walking with difficulty but thrilled, with her pocket full of my aunt's cash. Miriam would take her underwear off and empty the hidden pocket on our black table. I would watch Gaia gather the cash, count it, and then hurry to the neighborhood stores where she would buy food. It was too late in the afternoon for us to run to the open market. Miriam arrived home at dusk after the vendors had already left and the market had died down, leaving us with no time to walk across town to buy any discounted merchandise.

I was eight then, very shy and clumsy. When I asked Gaia if I could accompany Miriam to my aunt's store to bring home money, my sister laughed and promptly sewed a similar pocket onto my underpants. I was sent to the store with Miriam. I helped my sister but could not find any way to put the money into my pocket. I could not figure out how Miriam did it so easily. I felt every eye in the store on me all the time and at the end of the day, Miriam would walk home slowly with her pocket full. Mine was always empty.

On market day, at lunchtime, my uncle Macu often walked the short distance from the store to home for lunch. One day, he took me by the hand and asked me to walk home with him for a warm lunch and some cash. My aunt and uncle had no children of their own, and their house on Church Street was big and had a choking stench due to the many pieces of raw leather they bought and left lying around on the floor to finish drying. I dreamed of arriving home like Miriam, with money in my underpants pocket to dish out on our black table for Gaia to count and take to the store to buy food. Since I could not find a way to hide the money from my aunt's cash register, I thought I had a chance to get the needed money from my uncle. I followed him to his house.

There, my uncle led me into a bedroom with black furniture and a foul smell. He pulled his pants down, lay on the big bed, and took his penis out, telling me to play with it.

"Your aunt doesn't play with me anymore," he said. "I need some playing."

My uncle's penis looked like the huge, fat, and wrinkled earth worms that I played with in the backyard on rainy days after they were flushed out of their holes and were burned by the hot sun. I liked playing with the fresh worms in my backyard, and I sometimes dug them out of the ground and gave them to Gaia to cut up into small pieces and set the trail that attracted the neighbor's chickens into our kitchen. This one worm my uncle carried between his legs did not interest me, but I still touched it, as I was told. My only thought was bringing home money to buy food for the family. I do not remember if my uncle gave me the money that he had promised, but I never went back to the store with Miriam on Saturdays and never told my family the reason. Miriam proudly carried out her task for a long while and Nininha never noticed the missing cash. My sister stopped bringing money home much later, only after my aunt died and her husband could not keep the store.

It was also on Saturdays, at the end of the day, that Mother went to visit Dona Ervirinha, the blonde angel of my childhood. She was a tall and very generous woman who owned a farm and lived in a big house surrounded by a tall white wall, topped with pieces of colorful broken glass, a big yard and lots of tall trees full of aromatic flowers and fruit. Outside Dona Ervirinha's house, we would get in line with many other poor mothers along with their skinny, half-naked, big bellied and barefoot children for the weekly collection of the milk, ripe avocados, bananas, and colorful vegetables that Dona Ervirinha's employees had returned unsold from the market.

My younger brothers, Eduardo and Raimundo, and I would stay in line close to our mother. When it was our turn, the blonde and blue-eyed woman, like the angels I saw in church, would fill our basket with fruits and vegetables. She would give us extra pieces of meat, a big jar of coagulated milk that had been left out in the sun, and occasional bundles of used clothes and shoes. She would always talk to Mother for a bit.

"How are you and the children doing, Dona Raimunda?" she would ask.

"We're going along as God wills it, Dona Ervirinha," Mother would always answer.

"Come back here on Wednesday, and I'll gather some more clothes and shoes for you and the children, Dona Raimunda."

"Yes, Dona Ervirinha, and God will pay and protect you," Mother replied.

My brothers and I would help Mother carry the basket on our heads across town. We would return to Dona Ervirinha's house on Wednesdays for the extras and happily carry the gifts home.

Miuda was the brown angel of my childhood. She was the one angel that I did not see hanging from the ceiling and walls or holding candles at the altar of the town church, but who was of flesh and blood and whom I could touch and speak to. She lived next door to me. She was a black orphan of ten or eleven, severely malnourished—hence her nickname Miuda. She was small and was brought up by a crippled black woman, Dona Silvina. The young and the old depended upon each other almost entirely and earned a living by selling cooked cow and lamb intestines at the Saturday market. Dona Silvina's husband, João Sabino, would push the wheelbarrow all the way to the market on Saturdays, with his crippled wife holding onto the sides. Miuda would follow, pushing another squeaky wheelbarrow filled with pots and pans. The rest of the week, João Sabino would leave the house early in the morning and would come home drunk in the evening.

Dona Silvina wanted Miuda near her all of the time. The girl could not wander in the backyard for too long or distance herself too far from the eyes of her stepmother who yelled for her.

"Oh, Mi-u-da, hurry up and put more wood in the fire. Check the water in the pot," she would order.

"Oh, Mi-u-da, what're you doing now? Did you not hear me? Have you not done what I told you?" Dona Silvina would yell again and again when she did not see Miuda next to her.

"I'm gathering things for the market tomorrow," Miuda would yell back. "I'm coming right away."

Dona Silvina would send Miuda to buy lamb intestines at Seu Agemiro's slaughterhouse on the outskirts of town early morning. Miuda would carry the bloody organs on her head in a wooden basin that we called *gamela*. When she arrived, she would set the basin on the grass in the back of her house and clean the guts in the pond nearby. After the cleaning, Miuda would make small bundles of liver, coagulated blood, tongue, heart, and lung and wrap them in pieces of stomach sac tied with tripe, what we called *dobradinha*. In the afternoon, Miuda would cook the little bundles of delicacies in a black kettle on top of the black clay wood stove she had in her kitchen. Their kitchen wall was attached to the wall of our kitchen.

By late afternoon, after washing the intestines, the water in the pond behind Miuda's house would turn dark green with the dung dancing in the water, moving from side to side, according to the direction that the wind was blowing. Slowly, the muck would reach the edges of the pond, where it would stay and give off a profound sharp smell that enveloped the backyard and unsettled my soul.

I would stay far away from Miuda's green dung pond as much as possible and held my breath when I had to come into the house, but I would keep a close eye on the cooking of the guts. Their distinctive strong smell would invade our kitchen, overwhelm my senses and tempt my weak body.

Miuda's cooking troubled my siblings, too. It disturbed us most on Friday nights when the day had come and gone, and we remained with empty stomachs. Though Miuda would always find a way to hide some little bundles from her vigilant stepmother and pass them to Gaia's outstretched hands through the holes in our kitchen walls, there was never enough for the many dry mouths and shrunken stomachs in our house. Maybe it would have been better if Miuda had not given us anything at all, for once the little bit she gave Gaia hit our empty stomachs, our senses would wake up and transform us into ravaging hyenas.

Dona Silvina would never leave the side of her wood burning stove when the bundles were cooking on Friday afternoons. She would watch us. We would keep our eyes on her through the holes in our kitchen wall, too. We would wait for night to fall when Gaia quietly would remove the loose adobe blocks from the wall and help herself to Miuda's bundles.

After removing the blocks, my sister would slide her thin body through the small holes and enter Dona Silvina's dark kitchen. We would pass her our bucket, which she gave back to us through the holes with the warm *dobradinhas*. We were quick to carefully replace the dirt blocks and then would sit on the kitchen floor in the middle of the night devouring in no time the entrails Miuda had spent the whole day preparing.

Miuda knew we stole her bundles at night, but she would continue in her role as our accomplice and friend during the day. Dona Silvina suspected the girl handed us some of her food and sometimes beat her. She knew we entered her kitchen to steal her food and cursed the dirty starving thieves in the morning from her wheelchair when Gaia had gone too far by taking too many *dobradinhas*. But the beating, yelling, and cursing never stopped Miuda from helping us or Gaia from removing the loose blocks in the kitchen wall again and again when we had gone hungry. Gaia would make Miuda some cloth dolls for her to play with as a way of thanking her for alleviating our hunger.

Eduardo, a little over a year younger than me, was busy and practical, looking for ways to bring home food. He liked the freedom that the life he lived gave him: playing in our open backyard until dark, selling Mother's couscous and my sisters' panties and brassieres at our window and at the Suerdieck tobacco factory, hunting snakes for their skins, and killing birds for food with his slingshot. His stay at school was short, like most of my siblings. He dropped out after second grade. Eduardo was a good conversationalist, extremely verbal, quick, cute, thin, and never shy. He loved to talk and could sell anything or make any deal. So Mother would send him on visits to the townspeople when there was nothing in our house to eat. I often followed him to the center of town to the homes that we frequently visited.

We would cross the open soccer field and pass the town's big shower house where tired donkeys waited by the curb to be loaded with heavy wooden barrels of water that would be sold around town. I would hear the men whistling and singing their favorite tunes in the shower house while bathing. We would arrive at a house, surrounded by tall white walls with pieces of broken colored glass cemented to the top. The shards reflected kaleidoscopic colors and shapes, as the rays of the sun hit them at midday. Eduardo would knock at the tall gate door with a rock. After a few tries, the maid would come and lead us to the kitchen where the owner of the house, an elegant and pretty woman, Dona Bete, met us. She would take Eduardo by his hand and sit him on her lap, running her fingers through his tight curls and rubbing his skinny arms while I stood beside my brother and watched. Dona Bete would never say much to me. I knew she liked Eduardo. After a while, she would ask the maid to feed us. We would eat and drink sweet pineapple juice and sit quietly at the kitchen table. Sometimes, we were sent home with bags of avocados, dried meat, beans, rice, and old clothes and shoes. We would return to Dona Bete's house many more times when our mother sent us. My sisters said that the pretty owner of the big house had no children and her husband was always traveling.

My brother Carlos, whom we called Tatai, the fifth born in our family, was short and very husky at age fourteen when Father died. Soon after, Tatai would get up with the roosters at dawn to meet with Francisco, a well-known hunter in town. They walked to the arid area and hills that surrounded town, about fifteen miles away, to catch boa constrictors and chop wood. Tatai would arrive home at dusk, sweaty and puffy, carrying a huge dead boa wrapped around his neck or a bunch of wood piled on his head. He would kill the boa for us to eat and to sell its valuable skin at the market. I would watch Tatai set the dead snake on a bed of banana leaves in the backyard, sharpen our shiny kitchen knife on the black rock and carefully skin the snake. He would open its belly first and throw the guts to the pigs and chickens. He would pull off the skin from one end while we held on to the other. Then Tatai would salt the meat, briskly drying it over a big fire we would build to preserve the meat since we had no refrigeration. On Saturday, Tatai would take the snakeskin to the market, which he would sell to artisans who made drums and tambourines. My younger brothers, Eduardo and Raimundo, would follow him to the market, naked and hungry, to eat some of the manioc farina that the vendors spilled while filling the customers' bags. My younger brothers would wait, hopeful that Tatai would sell the snakeskin and with the money, buy some groceries to bring home. Tatai also sold the huge bundles of firewood he would bring home tied on his head with a rope when he could not catch boas. With any money earned, he would fill our black vine basket at the market in town. Gaia sometimes accompanied Tatai to the woods to help with the chopping, the carrying, and the selling of it door-to-door.

Our hardship was eased in other ways. Some days in December I would leave the house early in the morning and walk to the woods with my elder siblings to gather wild blackberries, which we called *quixaba*. I looked forward to these day trips. Upon arriving in the woods, we would search for the almost leafless prickly bushes, decorated with small black and sweet fruits. We would pull down the branches, quietly satisfy our appetites, fill our buckets and carry them home on our heads late in the afternoon when the cicadas' singing echoed in the air. Another juicy and round fruit, *umbú*, from the umbra tree, very common in our area, also helped fill us up.

We would climb tall cashew trees to pick fruits to bring home to eat. We would eat the succulent and meaty part of the fruit and save the nuts, which we would toast on a big tin sheet made from an empty kerosene drum. We cut the drum open, flattened it out, poked holes in the center, and place the nuts on it before setting the drum on a bonfire in the backyard. We would roast the nuts, turning them constantly with a long wooden stick until they were carbon dark on the outside. Then we would sit on the ground and crack them open on a rock. I loved the nuts. They were warm and delicious.

My siblings and I also would bring home from the woods a yellowish and prickly tropical fruit called *jaca*. The sweet layer inside the *jaca* had hidden large pits which we would save to eat later, cooked on our kerosene tin can on yet another fire. Sometimes we would gather the pits people had thrown on the street after eating the sweet part and bring them home to wash and cook. We also would climb the small palm trees to cut small bunches of a coconut-like fruit called *licurí*, which we would cook in the backyard. I loved the excitement of gathering wood and making these big fires.

At times, when my siblings had earned some money, we would get up with the roosters at daybreak. We would walk with our tin cups in one hand and a little sugar mixed with manioc farina in the other, to Seu Antonio Leone's corral, a big dairy farm in town, where cowboys milked their cows at dawn. We would arrive at the corral and wait, leaning quietly on the heavy wood fence, trying not to upset the farmer, the cows, or the cowboys. The scent of dried cow manure and fresh milk gave the corral a unique smell that is still deeply ingrained in my memory. It is a smell that is difficult to describe. There is nothing in the world like it. After a while, the cowboys would notice our presence and approach us, and without much ado, they would collect our tin cups and fill them with the foamy warm, sweet milk that we loved and had looked forward to. We then would sit on the ground near the corral, add the sweetened farina to the warm milk, and have a feast. The cowboys filled our tin cans with warm milk as many times as our stomachs would allow, and they blessed us. We would walk home with warm milk in our tin cans for our mother and a feeling of contentment as we met the rising sun on the horizon. That was the silver lining of our dark clouds.

Holly Day
Five Poems

Revision

on the timeline, I'm a map of wrong turns
detours—15, should have buried myself in computers
like my friends, at seventeen, should have buried myself in schoolwork,
taken advantage of my early college admittance, at nineteen
my father asks, you still think you're going to be
an astronaut? at twenty, lectures on how
real writers spend eight hours a day writing, not three
twenty-one, my boyfriend asks me how I can justify
spending so much money on postage to
send out manuscripts when I don't have anything
in the fridge.

I hear myself giving speeches on missed chances
to my children, to a son almost out of the house and I
know I've heard these lectures somewhere before, I hear myself tell my daughter
about how once upon a time all I wanted out of life was to
someday push an ice cream cart at the zoo
have a big, fat orange cat like the one sitting in my lap
children who loved me, and I think,
no, that's not exactly true.

For Now

every Halloween I get to see
a cavalcade of police cars in my yard, oh Midwest
police are so strong and steady, I know my
neighbors are glad to see them there. Oh no,
my best friend on TV just found a gun

now you should knock first before coming
in here. I know, I should have warned you that we were considering gun options
but lost all track of time in the shopping, the choosing.
I know, you and I, we were once so close we could have

exchanged skins, identities, but this new
friendly friend of mine, beamed flat and
bright on the screen from a station somewhere else
is company enough. He's more than enough.

The Things I Know

I read headlines about cannibals living in
plain sight, drunk driving accidents,
children bringing guns and knives and drugs to school and

I wonder how I'm supposed to send him out there
when five years old seems much too young to see this world.
I read headlines about priests charged with raping boys

daycare providers caught with child pornography
school janitors hiding secret murders for years
trusted neighbors with basement torture chambers, and

I wonder how they can ask me to let him go
when it seems my whole life has been about hiding
from the monsters waiting for us just beyond the door.

The Color of Your Breath

I don't need to
look when you call my
name your features
are fixed firmly in my
mind all of the
little expressions
that cross your face
when you're asleep the sound of
your footsteps as you
come up behind me

the smell
of your
skin this is all a part of
me now and even if
I was to go blind
I would still know what you
meant to me

The Night After the Picnic

flesh sears as his leg
drags across the red
hot metal of the
chrome tailpipe, skin peels
against the cool, rough concrete, leaves
red chunks all the way from sixty
to zero. fourth of july traffic
slows to
a crawl, then a stop,
everyone looking
at the four terrified kids out for
a drunk driving drive in daddy's car. daddy's
car, the new dent, how will they ever
explain the new dent? traffic slows, stops,
as rubbernecking
onlookers look
for the head of the boy from the accident,
lying headless, next to
his classic design scooter, lying in
a pool of endless blood,
blood so dark that the missing head
could be hiding just beneath the surface.
beneath the surface of the
thin pool, and no one
would ever know.
we wish it so.

Lee Gundersheimer

I Been There Before
A Play in One Act

The play takes place in two realities—a raft on the Mississippi River in the 1880's
which is actually in the middle of a family room of a lower middle-class home in Winona in the present day.
You'll see.

Cast of Characters:

LENORE—85 today, a long-ago retired English teacher battling a terminal illness

BILL—Late 30s, her son, a structural engineer, moved away at eighteen and rarely comes home.

ANN—two years older than her brother Bill, has never left Winona. A first-year middle school math teacher.

SCENE ONE

A woman in her eighties is standing on what might be a homemade raft of some sort. It should be crude, and it is not important at all that it can "float", though something about it has a wonderful magic or whimsy to it regardless. The main section of it is an old door. It has a cane with a wicker basket for an oar. Perhaps a sheet or a garbage bag, or a plastic table cloth, or a housecoat, for a sail, and one of those bathtub commodes to sit on with a large picnic basket for provisions. But behind this is a projection of a beautiful majestic video of the Mississippi River, floating down the river, the bluffs on either side. The water is calm, and you can hear the sounds of nature throughout. The women speaks as though it was the late 1880's even though she if from our time period.

LENORE: Okay, Lord, you listen up now, hear? I'm goin to make me sumpin like confession. I'm gonna ask you just once now to forgive me and then it's up to you. I know you can hear me. Don't make no difference you and me don't know each other much. I knew you was always there. Just want you to know one thing, and then you can get on back to your business. I done something that you might not like. That you might think ain't right. Took me some money, that didn't belong to me. But I didn't steal it. Just found it. Lyin right by a man that was killed. Murdered. And I didn't have nothing to do with that none neither. He was killed by some other pretty bad people, not me. But I guess if you bein who you are you done known that already, now don't you? Don't really understand this confessing thing then anyway. You already supposed to know all that happened, done caused it to happen, so then why do folks think they need to explain it all over again to ya'll? I suppose it's the admitting it then. Recognizing they done something right or wrong. Well, I'm just a boy, and I don't know much about all that. Have me a drunk for a Pa, so is that right or wrong? No Ma to speak of, no real home most days, is that right or wrong? I smoke me my cigarettes, and let loose me a few swear words every now and then, is that right or wrong? What do I know about anything, when it comes right down to it. This whole damn mess confuses me each and evry day. So what am I supposed to do with that, Mr. Lord? What am I supposed to do with it? Lived on this dern river my whole life. Thirteen years now. Ain't never been out on it. Not once. Never had me a boat. Now I am actually right out on it. In the middle of it. See when it come time for me to make my gettaway, well it done make perfect sense to sail on outta here. Ain't nobody gonna look for me out here. Not on the mighty Mississippi. And it worked. Plum near everyone in town musta be lookin for me. I seen their lanterns and heard them callin. Huck! Huckleberry! Huck Finn! You come back here now. Where is you? Huck! Well hell, they never worried much for me when I was back there among 'em, so why make such a racket when I don't turn up for supper? They musta known I got all this here money. They musta found out and want some for themselves. Well, they didn't find it, I did. Me. So it's mine. Nobody give me the time of day before, cept when they need somethin, or when my Pa takes to drink and just wants to whip me for spite. Well its just me now. Me and this here river. Your river. You, Mr. Lord, and me, and this here river. We gonna be great friends. Look at her. Damn sure's pretty as a picture.

The lights begin to crossfade.

SCENE TWO

The projection of the river is blurring, slowly fading from view and transforming into the bad wallpaper of a midwest family room. We hear just a voice first, then another.

BILL: Mom? Mom?

ANN: She won't hear you, BILL.

BILL: She's not deaf. Yet. Is she?

ANN: No. She just doesn't answer to her name anymore.

A man in his late thirties and woman a few years older are standing near the "raft" and it is clearly just sitting in a room now, no longer floating down the river. If possible, what looked almost magical before looks kind of sad and pathetic, makeshift. There is part of a kitchen area to one side.

BILL: I'm not calling her by name. Her name is Lenore. I'm calling her Mom. Mom?

ANN: Her name is Huckleberry now.

BILL: What?

ANN: Huckleberry-

BILL: Really—

ANN: Like Huckleberry Finn.

BILL: Thank you. And here, I thought it was Huckleberry, like Huckleberry Hound. I know who Huckleberry Finn is thank you.

ANN: Oh, did you actually make it to school that day?

BILL: Mom, how can you be Huckleberry Finn? He was a boy. (to ANN) Wasn't he?

ANN: You did read the book, then. That makes how many, one?

BILL: Of course, I read it. Who hasn't read Huck Finn? I must have at some point. Goes on the river, right? In a raft. Oh my god, is that what this is? Her raft?

ANN: Yes.

BILL: Mom, that is an old door. Your sitting on the old door to the kitchen, not a raft.

ANN: She doesn't care Bill. She believes what she wants to believe now.

BILL: You must have done this. Put this here. She couldn't have done this herself. Why do you keep doing this shit? Why let her get away with this?

ANN: Get away? What is she getting away with?

BILL: The last time it was stealing candy from the Woolworth's was it not? Swedish Fish?

ANN: Walgreens, Bill. There hasn't been Woolworth's for ages. And she wanted to do it, said it would be fun. She did it once when she was little. With her friend

BILL: Who, Tom Sawyer? No wait she was still a girl back then, so it must have been- what was the girl's name. Betsy?

ANN: Becky.

BILL: Hatcher

ANN: Thatcher.

BILL: Mom told me she got caught, you both got caught, stealing from the candy counter at Woolworths. That's what she told me.

ANN: It was Walgreens. But yes, it was Swedish Fish. She's had chemo, Bill. And fifteen rounds of radiation. She's been to death's door and back, if she wants to

BILL: Become a felon, aided and abetted by her own daughter—

ANN: Stealing Swedish Fish is not a felony. Even in Minnesota. They thought it was charming. When I explained to them, and once I had paid for it.
BILL: I heard you are not even allowed in the store anymore. Which is kind of regretful because she is a cancer patient, and it is the closest drug store.

ANN: They're overpriced anyway. We prefer Goltz's. Look if Mom-

BILL: Mom, where's Mom. I don't see our Mom anywhere in this room!

ANN: If she wants to raft down my family room floor as a runaway boy, why the hell not?

BILL: Her family room floor. Her floor. Not yours. You don't have a family room floor, Ann. Not yet anyway. Hey, Huckleberry, I hate to break it to you, but you're a girl, not a boy. And not a girl really, a woman, an old woman. 85. Today. I drove five hours in the fricking snow because it's your birthday. And I brought you this. Do you want to open it? It's a present. For you. Here, I'll open it for you. Do you want me to do that? Okay, here, I will. It's like, a slanket or something like that. See, a blanket with sleeves. For when you're watching T.V. and shit. Teresa knitted it for you. She says they are very hard to make. Something about the shape. Lots of seams.

ANN: They call them snuggies, Bill. Not whatever you just called it?

BILL: It's what Teresa called it, not me. A slanket. Like a blanket with sleeves. What is a snuggie? A nugget with sleeves?

ANN: That's what they're actually called in Kmart or Walmart or whatever fine Marts actually sells those priceless things.

BILL: Up yours, Ann. She knitted this herself. For Mom. She was operating under the misguided notion our mother was still an old lady, who might get chilly and want to wrap herself up and read on the sofa, not some runaway, roustabout rafting up river.

ANN: Wow. Must have had lots of R's to use up in Words With Friends.

BILL: *Under his breath.* Jesus—

ANN: Looks like it is helping with your usually near Neanderthal vocabulary.

BILL: Fuck you.

ANN: I take it back. And so should Teresa.

BILL: She made it, Ann. Herself. You can't take it back.

ANN: Too bad.

BILL: Don't be such a bitch. Oh, I'm sorry, that's what you do. Probably for a living now.

ANN: Trust me, if I could I would. No one will pay you for it. To be *their* bitch, sure, but not to just bitch. Unless you're a nun. Do they even get paid?

LENORE: Dern this wind. It's done blown me off my course here.

BILL: Mom, this is for you. Teresa made it for you.

ANN: Herself. So you can't take it back. No gift receipt.

BILL: Ann—

ANN: Speaking of bitch where is Teresa anyway?

BILL: She didn't come.

ANN: Well that's obvious, Bill. I didn't think you left her in the car.

BILL: She has a conference.

ANN: I'm sure.

BILL: In the cities. It's a big once a year thing.

ANN: At New Years? Ringing in the New Year at a conference?

BILL: The conference starts on the second. The second through the fourth.

ANN: Who has a once a year conference during the holidays. Apparently shoe clerks do. What is a conference for shoe clerks like? Breakout sessions on who the hell is stupid enough to buy those wedges?

BILL: She's not a shoe clerk, she is a manager of the second largest shop in the state.

ANN: Multiple degrees from almost every grad school in the country landed her the second largest DSW in Minnesota? That must have made her mother proud.

BILL: And what are you now, middle school math teacher, and a mid-semester replacement at that? I guess that gives you bragging rights?

ANN: Ouch. *(pause)* Bitch.

BILL: Learned from the best.

ANN: You mean there was one thing I didn't suck at according to you?

BILL: There are many things you don't suck at, Ann. I'm not the one who doesn't have any confidence in you. You cornered that market yourself.

ANN: Mom was a teacher, Bill. She was very happy I took the job.

BILL: She was probably happy you got a job. After mooching off of her for what twenty years. And she was an English teacher, not math. She hated math.

ANN: So did you.

BILL: So does everyone with any sense.

ANN: Wow, probably not good for a structural engineer to hate math.

LENORE: We need to steer away from them shoals. Or we're a gonna crack up here. Gimme that rope.

BILL: Not much of a rope here, Huck

ANN: I don't know it has a sort of Found Art charm.

BILL: It's a slanket, Mom.

LENORE: Give her to me. We gotta cast off outta here while that southwestern wind is blowin.

ANN: Give it to her. Bill, you brought the damn thing for her, give it to her. What are you going to say when Teresa asks if she liked it?

BILL: Here, Mom. Happy Birthday. From both of us.

LENORE: Good. Just in time. Now back off. Don't want them to find me.

She tosses the slanket as far as she can.

LENORE: Time to get me the hell on outta here.

Blackout

SCENE THREE

The river. Dawn.

LENORE: Funny thing about being alone. It's scary first innit ? Damn scary. The sound of your heart. Thoughts swirlin inside your head. Feels dark, even in broad daylight. Terrifying. Then just like this river here, you let things be, jus paddle along, and I be damned if it don't get to be all shiney like, and calm. You find yourself glidin along. No one to worry about. Not a care in this whole wide world. Don't gotta be home to help with chores. Don't gotta worry bout what time to get to bed. Heck, you want to take a nap, you just take yourself a nap. Work? What in the heck is that anyway? Work. *(She pretends to spit into the river in disdain.)* That's just somethin grown-ups tell you you need to do to make you some money. It always have to come down to money. Well I got me some money now, first time in my life, and let me tell you somethin. I ain't a scared of nothin no more.

SCENE FOUR

The family room. Later the same morning.

BILL: *Coming from the kitchen.* You don't have any coffee, Ann?

ANN: I don't drink it.

BILL: Not even for company?

ANN: We don't have much company these days.

BILL: No, I suppose not. Not on the set of Castaway here.

ANN: And who knew you were even going to show up. Let alone when.

BILL: How long has this been going on?

ANN: Just after Thanksgiving, I think. Not long. Right after her last treatment. I thought talking to her about the books she loved to teach might get her up off the the chair she was sitting in all day. The next day I found her sitting in the middle of the room on her commode paddling with her cane and talking like she was some kind of boy. It took me a few minutes to figure out who she was. I should have guessed. Huck Finn was always her favorite semester.

BILL: She taught Tom Sawyer though. Not Huck Finn. Huck Finn was too racy.

ANN: Not racy, Racist. Because of the "n"- word. Got the folks on the school board's panties all up in knots. She tried to teach it one year. Because it was the better book. Or so she thought. Stubborn as a mule. Caused all that commotion, almost got her forced into early retirement. They warned her and she taught it anyway.

LENORE: Most folks ain't worth the dirt they's standing on, that's how I come to see it.

BILL: So she talks to you from time to time? Even though she is paddling down the Mississippi?

ANN: She's talking to the river. Nothing about it is logical, Bill. You can't look for the logic in it.

BILL
Not in this house. I learned that lesson long ago. Does she stay on that thing all day?

ANN:
Yes.

BILL: What about at night?

ANN: She just gets up and goes to bed.

BILL: Does she at least pull over and tie up the raft?

ANN: Bill, look the whole thing doesn't make any sense. When I get up she is already out here-

BILL: Sailing on down the river.

ANN: I even got up early one morning, it was Christmas I think, and she walked out here with her walker, made her tea-

BILL: You have tea? Why didn't you say so?

ANN: You didn't ask. Top cupboard. She made her tea and toast. And she just got onboard to eat it.

BILL: *Yelling from kitchen.* Onboard.

ANN: You know what I mean. And that's when I realized it is like reading a book. You pick it up and put it down. But when you are reading it, it has become your world.

BILL: *Returning after putting tea kettle on stove.* So she thinks she is reading a book.

ANN: Not exactly, more like living in it.

BILL: And she has been doing this for over a month. And you helped her.

ANN: Well, it seemed like a pretty nice thing to do. We didn't exchange presents this year. We can't. We don't have any money left. Probably going to end owing owe thousands. Couldn't even afford a tree. First time ever … our whole lives we always managed to celebrate. At least at Christmas.

BILL: And what a farce that was most years.

ANN: Yeah, but once a year we were a family. For at least those few days. Lights and ornaments. You even loved the tinsel. Used to stick it in between your teeth.

BILL: To blow on it like streamers. You know like in a fan or air conditioner. *He demonstrates feebly.*

ANN: I was there. It was not like I thought you wanted to floss with it. So I thought why not give Mom this. *Gesturing to the raft.* Make her something. The door was in the basement.

BILL: *From kitchen again.* I know it was from the kitchen. I remember when he kicked it down.

ANN: We didn't have any money and it was the holidays. I wanted to give her something.

BILL: *Returning.* Too bad she wasn't reading the Great Gatsby.

ANN: What harm is it doing. She is the most alive I have seen her in years.

BILL: Yeah, until she decides to switch to Last of the Mohicans.

ANN: I am not wanting her to die, Bill.

BILL: I never said that.

ANN: Yes, you did. Not yet anyway, you said. About the house, about the family room. I know this isn't my house. I know you and Teresa are going to fight me for it. For your share of it. I am perfectly aware of that.

BILL: Stop it, Ann. We are not going to fight you for anything,

ANN: Bullshit. That's why you are here, isn't it?

BILL: I came for the tea. And for Mom's birthday.

ANN: We never see you but what, once or twice a year. Just enough to be the dutiful son, to protect your share of the old family homestead.

BILL: Yeah, cause it fills me with such warm memories, cozy fireside beatings from dad … Ann, we have talked about this all, years ago. It was settled. We would split it all fairly—no Shakespearean bullshit. I told you you were crazy to stay here, to get the hell out.

ANN: Not everyone is you, Bill.

BILL: What is that even supposed to mean? Now you are going to give me crap, because I found a way to survive? Look if you want to stay in this nightmare of a home, you go right ahead. We both know what it is doing to you. What it did to you. And Mom. I mean look at her? I'm just thankful I had the balls to get out when I did. And I never took one dollar. Not from Mom or the twenty cents Dad left her once he thankfully finally died. I paid my way through school. I earned every dime I ever made.

ANN: But now you want your share. Of the place you said you couldn't wait to get away from.

BILL: Why are you doing this? We settled this years ago. We calmly talked about it. You get your share, and I get my share.

ANN: And don't forget, dear little Roger gets his.
BILL: He's her only grandson. It was Mom's idea to split it three ways, Not mine.

ANN: After you took her to that stupid graduation. How do you even graduate from home schooling anyway?

BILL: It is very rigorous schooling, Ann.

ANN: Oh, I'm sure.

BILL: There are regulations. You earn a degree, a diploma.

ANN: What do you print it out on your home computer? And did it ever occur to you that it might piss your own mother off, who worked for forty-eight years in the public-school system, that you and Teresa decided to home school Roger?

BILL: He's a good kid, it worked out just fine for him.

ANN: Yeah, where is he living now? Some forest in Washington?

BILL: He's an environmentalist. An environmental activist.

ANN: He's a mixed up stupidly, optimistic kid, dumpster diving for food with no idea what to do with his life, Bill. Trust me, I know the type. Intimately.

BILL: Is this about Roger? Is all this anger about Roger being given a share of Mom's inheritance?

ANN: No that would be too Shakespearean.

BILL: Don't give her any ideas, please Mark Twain is bad enough.

ANN: You don't have a clue, do you. You never did. Well it's no longer Mom's birthday, so do what you do best, pack up and leave.

BILL: I thought I would stay for New Years. With you and Huck Finn here.

ANN: We don't do New Years, Bill. Never have. No need for yet another reason to drink. Like Mom always said Hell is paved with New Year's resolutions.

BILL: Mark Twain said that not, Mom. I mean she said it because he did. "New Years is the time to make all your resolutions", was the saying,

ANN & BILL: "because next week you can start paving Hell with them as usual." *They share a laugh at both having been fed the quote enough to remember it.*

BILL: You know for a supposedly funny man, he was one depressing dude.

ANN: "Sanity and happiness are an impossible combination."

ANN & BILL: "No sane man can be happy, for to him—"

ANN: "life is real, and he sees what a fearful thing it is."

ANN & BILL: "Only the mad can be happy—"

ANN: "and not many of those." That was always one of my favorites.

BILL: Like I said, the laughs just keep coming. Don't they give out like a comedy prize with his name on it? The Mark Twain prize? They ought to call it the Mark Twain curse. So let's repave the way to hell tonight together, what do you say? Not a good night to be alone, New Years.

ANN: You two had a fight, didn't you, Bill? *He does not say anything.* Oh, Christ. That is why you are even here. You never could tell a good lie. Well, so are you guys alright? Was it a real blood and guts no holds barred, or just a "dammit, If you don't like the sweater vest, just take it back.

BILL: I'm not sure. And is that how you think married people fight? Over sweater vests?

ANN: Who else even buys them? They are like unfinished sweaters. Every time I see them, I wonder if you can buy the sweater sleeves in another part of the store. Answer the question.

BILL: Yes, you can buy sweater sleeves, they call them leg warmers. We haven't been doing well for a while now.

ANN: Try your whole marriage. Well, tell me I'm wrong, and I'll shut up.

BILL: That has never once worked-

ANN: What your marriage or me shutting up?

BILL: You admitting you were wrong.

ANN: True, though why lie, I never have been. Look, Bill, it should come as no surprise that you and Rin-Tin-Teresa are not soul-mates. She didn't even like your own wedding. And she planned it. How is Rodger, did he come home for the holidays?

BILL: He's fine. He's actually visiting her parents. For a week. In Boca Raton.

ANN: Which I can only assume is in Florida. What does that mean anyway, the mouth of the rat?

BILL: What is this tea anyway?

ANN: Sleepytime. Thought it might help her rest. Who calls a town Rat Mouth?

BILL: Tastes like cat pee.

ANN: Boca Raton or the tea? Put some honey in it. Then it will taste like cat pee with honey. So is Teresa even going to a shoe clerk conference?

BILL: Yes, in February right now she's flying down to Rat Mouth to see Rodger and her parents. Left yesterday, did not even ask if I wanted to go. Let's just say it does not seem hopeful.

ANN: Sounds like you hit the lottery to me. No New Years in Rat Mouth with the Republicans.

BILL: I'm not sure either of us have enough skin left in the game.

ANN: That is an unfortunate metaphor on many levels.

BILL: Not like I would even know a healthy relationship if it kicked me square in the nutsack, so what do you expect.

ANN: Those are the exact words the great poets of yore often used.

BILL: Look at from whence we were raised. So is it okay to stay and have our own New Year's Eve gala? And I resolve to make not even one single resolution? I brought champagne and everything.

ANN: *Laughs to herself.* You got to make allowances. It's the way we're raised.

BILL: Now that one I do remember. "Kings is kings," right? And that one is from Huckleberry Finn.

LENORE: "All I say is, kings is kings, and you got to make allowances. Take them all around, they're a mighty ornery lot. It's the way they're raised."

As Bill goes to his overnight bag to take out a bottle of champagne, Lenore gets down from the chair on the raft and grabs a walker and begins to shuffle into her bedroom.

BILL: Is she going to sleep? It's like 9:30 in the morning.

ANN: Probably going to the bathroom. All that talk of cat piss and tea.

BILL: Hey, Mom. You need help?

ANN: Bill—

BILL: You want some help?

ANN: Be careful!

Lenore alarmed at his touch wheels around-

LENORE: No, sir!

The startled motion she makes hits Bill, causing the champagne bottle to fall from his hand and go crashing to the floor.

ANN: She doesn't like to be touched anymore.

Lenore does not even react to the broken bottle and continues to shuffle out of the room.

BILL: She never like to be touched.

The lights fade as they begin to clean up the broken bottle and spilled wine.

ANN: A might ornery lot.

BILL: That bastard Twain was wrong, hell is paved with attempts at kindness.

Lights Fade.

SCENE FIVE

Almost midnight later that night. The family room. We hear the sound of a television, but it is on the fourth wall, so we only hear it. New Year's Rockin Eve. Bill is curled up in an arm chair, not even watching it. He is reading of all things "Huckleberry Finn." He is drinking a bottle of beer. Two more are at his feet.

BILL: *Reading from the book.* "And then Tom he talked along and talked along, and says, lee's all three slide out of here one of these nights and get an outfit, and go for howling adventures amongst the Injuns, over in the Territory, for a couple of weeks or two; and I says, all right, that suits me, but I ain't got no money for to buy the outfit, and I reckon I couldn't get none from home, because it's likely pap's been back before now, and got it all away from Judge Thatcher and drunk it up. "No, he hain't," Tom says; "it's all there yet—six thousand dollars and more; and your pap hain't ever been back since. Hadn't when I come away, anyhow." Jim says, kind of solemn: "He ain't a-comin' back no mo', Huck." I says: Why, Jim?" "Nemmine why, Huck—but he ain't comin' back no mo." But I kept at him; so at last he says: "Doan' you 'member de house dat was float'n down de river, en dey wuz a man in dah, kivered up, en I went in en unkivered him and didn' let you come in? Well, den, you kin git yo' money when you wants it, kase dat wuz him." Tom's most well now, and got his bullet around his neck on a watch-guard for a watch, and is always seeing what time it is, and so there ain't nothing more to write about, and I am rotten glad of it, because if I'd a knowed what a trouble it was to make a book I wouldn't a tackled it, and ain't a-going to no more. But I reckon I got to light out for the Territory ahead of the rest, because Aunt Sally, she's going to adopt me and sivilize me, and I can't stand it. I been there before. The end. Yours truly, Huck Finn." What? Is that actually the end of the damn thing? I been there before, the end? Yours truly?

Ann enters carrying two unmatched suitcases.

BILL: They call this the Great American novel and it actually sucks. I mean certainly the end. And the

whole time Jim was free, so all of the crap that happens to them, it didn't even have to have happened. He wasn't even technically a runaway slave.

ANN: But they don't know that.

BILL: That's a technicality.

ANN: So if Huck thinks he is going to hell, and is doing things that are terrible and wrong, it doesn't matter if they are fact, or truthful, or even necessary. Twain is saying that in reality, the reality is not important.

BILL: Look Kafka, all I am saying is that it isn't satisfying. If that is even what he meant and is just not your ironic-over-intellectualizing-a flawed-ending-into-more-than-the sum-of-its-suckiness. I'm just saying it's worse than Hitchcock's Birds. The end of the whole damn thing, of the supposed best book every written is let me light on out of here for the Territory and rassle with some Injuns. Not exactly "so we beat on, boats against the current, born back ceaselessly into the past."

ANN: All your point of view, I guess. Boats as metaphor for life, yeah, okay both have that. And is ceaselessly even a word?

BILL: Where are you going?

ANN: And being born back into the past is over-rated is that not what you always tell me?

BILL: Ann, it is almost midnight, on New Year's Eve, where in the hell are you going?

ANN: I thought I'd go for a vacation. Grand Canyon. Maybe Niagara Falls, I don't know. Shouldn't be too hard to book a ticket. Not tonight. I have a week until the break is over. Oh, crap, why lie. I'm so tired of all the deception.

BILL: Now we sound like Tennessee Williams.

ANN: You can't pray a lie. Isn't that what Mamma always said. You aren't the only one with secrets. I am at liberty, or so it seems. Winona Middle School asked me to not come back. Turns out teaching is not one of my strong suits either. And so I am to be replaced by another midterm replacement.

BILL: Oh, Ann, I am so sorry. Can you fight it. Can you go to the unions or the teacher's association or whatever?

ANN: Apparently being a few hours late a few times in a row, for a few weeks now, is not setting strong model behavior for middle school minds.

BILL: Late? How late?

ANN: Oh sometimes, midday, sometime the next day.

BILL: Why?

ANN: Because the Mississippi here was flooding my family room, and sometimes I just felt like I was drowning, and who knows. Why? Because I have a mother who has not even a little toe left in reality, and so sometimes it was hard to shave my legs and hook up my bra and get on out of here on time. Because even though I love math, the beautiful precision of each decimal of it- I truly can make any equation even out equal on the chalkboard, but I just can't seem to find the same-oh damn, the only word I can come up with, so forgive the trite obviousness of it—is balance. I can't seem to find the balance in the mundane day-to-dayness of it all. Maybe I should try Boca Raton? No I'm not that fucking crazy, not yet.

BILL: I thought you were broke?

ANN: Not yet, technically. Isn't that what flawless credit is for?

BILL: But what about Mom?

ANN: What about her?

BILL: I mean—

ANN: Who's going to make sure she doesn't piss herself, and eats her Ensure, and pulls the hairs from her chin so she won't look like a old crone? That is just going to have to be your gig for the time being. It's not like you have pressing family obligations back in St. Cloud.

BILL: I have a job.

ANN: So did I, I made do.

BILL: Apparently not.

ANN: "I don't like work even when someone else is doing it."

BILL: Please, can we stop the quoting of Mark Goddamn Twain!

ANN: How do you know it was his?

BILL: Because if it sounds like a tee shirt or a carved patio stone it must be his. I never realized we grew up in a sort of shrine to Mark Twain. And now it seems, it's a literal one.

ANN: There is more tea under the sink. And actually a whole case of wine in the hallway closet. I just didn't want Mom to see it.

BILL: Where are you—when are you—coming back?

ANN: I don't know. This is unchartered territory for me.

Lenore appears in the doorway. She is shuffling toward the raft. The countdown to New Years can be heard. 40- 39, 38.

BILL: You can't just leave, Ann

ANN: You did.

BILL: I was seventeen. I was a stupid mixed up hurt kid.

ANN: And how old was I, Bill? I was 20.

The TV countdown continues, 19, 18, 17, 16….

BILL: This is crazy.

ANN: "When we remember we are all mad, the mysteries disappear, and life stands explained."

BILL: *He has turned, distracted by the TV countdown now.* If you tell me that was Mark Twain, I am going to—

5, 4, 3, 2, 1. Bill is watching the TV and all of the shouting "Happy New Year. Happy New Year!" He doesn't see Ann leave. He turns back to say-

BILL: Happy New Year.

But she is gone. He is about to run out the door to try and stop her when Lenore yells—

LENORE: "He ain't a-comin' back no mo', Huck." He ain't a-coming back no mo'.

Bill is startled and doesn't know what to do.

LENORE: "He ain't a-comin' back no mo', Huck." He ain't a-coming back no mo'.

BILL: *Slowly remembering this part of the book.* "Why, Jim?"

LENORE: "Nemmine why, Huck—but he ain't comin' back no mo."

BILL: *Goes over to the chair and picks up the book and carries it on the raft and sits on the picnic basket next to his mother and reads his part. The projection of the Mississippi slowly starts to come into view and is complete by the end of the play.* But I kept at him; so at last he says:

LENORE: "Doan' you 'member de house dat was float'n down de river, en dey wuz a man in dah, kivered up, en I went in en unkivered him and didn' let you come in? Well, den, you kin git yo' money when you wants it, kase dat wuz him."

BILL: R*reading.* Tom's most well now, and got his bullet around his neck on a watch-guard for a watch, and is always seeing what time it is, and so there ain't nothing more to write about, and I am rotten glad of it, because if I'd a knowed what a trouble it was to make a book I wouldn't a tackled it, and ain't a-going to no more.
Lenore touches his shoulder and rests her hand on it.

LENORE & BILL: But I reckon I got to light out for the Territory ahead of the rest …

BILL: … because Aunt Sally she's going to adopt me and sivilize me, and I can't stand it.

LENORE & BILL: I been there before.

BILL: The End.

LENORE: Yours Truly, Huck Finn.

Christopher G. Bremicker
Welch Village

I waited for my brother to pick me up. We were going downhill skiing at an area one hour south of St. Paul, past Hastings, where I spent six months in a veterans' home before moving to the hi-rise where I now lived. We loved to ski and did it all our lives. My building manager looked at my skis propped in a bag by the front door. She looked at me in my ski parka and helmet, as my brother pulled in. She stifled a laugh.

I must have been a sight. People who lived in hi-rises were not downhill skiers. The sport was second only to polo in expense. I was not going to let poverty keep me from skiing.

My brother was buying the lift tickets. I paid for my own lunch and bought coffee for both of us. He supplied the car and gasoline. My lift ticket was his Christmas gift to me.

"Don't hurt yourself," my manager advised, as I hoisted my skis onto my shoulder and left the building. I was seventy years old and people expected me to be in a rocking chair. Many men who were my age were in wheelchairs, especially at the veterans' hospital, where I got my medical care. I opened the back door of my brother's SUV, slid my skis on top of his, and threw in my boot-bag.

I placed the ski helmet gingerly onto the boot bag. Despite its construction to withstand impact, the helmet's inner workings were fragile. The helmet had stereo speakers I connected to an MP3 player that played Mozart, Beethoven, Bach, and the Rolling Stones, as I descended the hill in a series of turns, I tried to link and make graceful. The Stones pounded *Brown Sugar* into my brain as I drove my knees into each turn and wedeled down the hill. Beethoven's *Moonlight Sonata* was background music for the day.

I bought the helmet at the end of the season, half price. The salesman at Joe's Sporting Goods, who was seventy years old, took his time fitting me. He knew his stuff. The helmet was called a Demon.

I bought the skis with a check from my dead mother's telephone bill account. The telephone cooperative in my hometown sent our family a refund and I used it to buy the same skis used by the Vail Ski Patrol. They were Atomics, gray in color.

I bought the boots end of season, too, with a tax rebate. Half price, they were three hundred and fifty dollars. I had them ten years and they were as functional, and fashionable, as the day I bought them. They were bright red, Nordica boots. Skiing equipment was extremely expensive. My mother always objected that it became obsolete the year after a person bought it. That was true, and a three-hundred-dollar ski parka was out of fashion the next year. A pair of skis, with the latest technology and graphics, was obsolete the next year, too.

So, with our equipment in the back of the car, my brother and I drove out of St. Paul, along the freeway that went through downtown, past the railroad yards, into the farmland that was exorbitantly priced because it was so close to the Cities. We followed the Mississippi River to Hastings. The river was beginning to open and there was a channel of water down its center.

Hastings brought back memories. We passed the Perkins Restaurant where my uncle bought me lunch when I lived at the veterans' home and he drove down from St. Paul to go over a story I wrote. We passed the restaurant where I had coffee at its counter to get out of the home. We passed the drug store where I escaped every day and the A.A. club where I cut my teeth in that Society.

We took a gradual left turn after Hastings and entered an area of small houses interspersed in farmland. They had large lawns. People lived there and commuted to the Cities.

I asked my brother if he could live there and he said, he could. I said, the isolation would drive me crazy. I needed the proximity of people to keep me sane.

Then we entered an area of pure farmland, where the fields were barren with snow, the barbed wire fences hung in disrepair, and little farmhouses were next to barns that looked a hundred years old. Geese were in fields. Crows pecked at seeds in the farrow.

We took a left onto a freeway that led to Red Wing. I remembered the Sheldon Theater in Red Wing that we visited when I was at the veterans' home. We saw a musical about Patsy Cline, the country western singer, whose plane crashed, killing her at a young age. My mother had a Patsy Cline album in her record collection.

I remembered the cinnamon rolls and coffee we got at a restaurant before the show. I remembered the visit we made to Stillwater State Prison to take an A.A. meeting to the inmates. I was terrified when our guide asked us if anyone wanted to spend the night.

We followed the freeway a mile or two then turned right at an old church with a cemetery. We followed this road into a canyon. It wound through woods and, as we descended, the farmland rose behind us. We came to a village at the base of this canyon. It had a mill, post office, bar, general store, and a bed and breakfast. This was Welch Village and the ski area, which rose above the canyon, was a mile down the road.

The Cannon River ran through Welch Village and created the canyon above which we skied. A sign on the mill advertised inner tubing on the river. I was told the river had trout.

We pulled into the parking lot of the ski area. It was a prodigious parking lot, with room for more cars in a muddy field across the road, and there were many cars parked there already. It would be a busy day. We hoped, on the drive down, that the ski racers would not be there, but their buses were lined up in the lot like school buses at a high school, dropping off students. Racers took over the chalet. Their parents drove down, too, and there was no place to leave our boot bags, let alone sit down and eat.

We parked and carried our stuff across the frozen puddles of the lot to the chalet, where we leaned our skis and poles against a picnic table out front. My brother went into the chalet to buy the lift tickets. I took my stuff upstairs to the same part of the chalet we always used, next to the window that stuck out by the deck that faced the hill.

And hill it was. If a skier was used to skiing in the mountains, this was Midwest skiing. It was Midwest skiing at its best, but the vertical drop was only a few hundred feet. The vertical drop at Vail, Colorado, for example, was in the thousands.

My brother appeared, and I bought coffee. A cup of coffee before putting on our boots was our ritual. We skied so many times, on so many hills and mountains, that we were in no rush to go out and do it again.

I didn't ski much these days, out of poverty and boredom with it, and my brother skied because it filled his days in retirement in the winter. He had nothing else to do. However, we were both outdoorsmen and leapt at a chance to get outside.

We put on our boots. Ski boots were notoriously tight, and we struggled to get them onto our feet. We buckled them shut with a vengeance. I heard that downhill racers, the skiers who reached eighty miles an hour on skis, clamped their feet into their boots so tightly they ached. My boots fit well, and I never had problems with coming off the slopes because my feet hurt.

We put on our helmets, goggles, and gloves. I turned on my MP3 player and placed it in the pocket of my parka. Then we clumped through the chalet, awkward in our boots, past skiers pulling on their boots, and opened the heavy wooden door.

We walked onto the deck that led to a metal, grated stairway with a railing which we held onto as we walked down. We clumped to our skis, retrieved them, carried them up the hill on the snow, toward the lift shed, and put them on. We put the leather straps on our poles around our wrists.

Our bindings were so safe these days that people did not break their legs. It was rare someone was tobogganed off the hill. It did happen, though, and everyone felt sorry for the person being cradled down the hill, held in check by ski patrolmen

holding ropes to keep the sled from sliding downhill. The skier was bundled in the sled like in a body bag.

My brother and I skated to the lift shed. This was a workout, I could feel it in my belly, and my muscles tightened with the exertion. However, it felt good to move and know I could still do this.

We poled onto the little platform the lift operator made with a shovel and got on the lift. The operator held the chair in place, as it swung around on the lift's big, overhead wheel and slid it under us. The chair swung for a moment, tilted toward a tower or two then stabilized and took us up the hill.

The chair ascended a swath cut between the trees. This was the closest we got to nature, as we looked around us, at the ski hill, the chalet, parking lot, and the Cannon River below us. Woods were on both sides.

The crisp air bit our noses. We did not wear hats, but our ski helmets kept us warm. We wore long underwear, which we wished we left at home, as the day progressed.

I listened to Fleetwood Mac's "You Can Go Your Own Way." My brother told me stories about the Minnesota Department of Natural Resources, from which he was recently retired. I listened to the music in the helmet and heard him talk at the same time.

He told me about the National Rifle Association and how its ranks were corrupted from a pro hunting organization to a bunch of cowboys who liked assault weapons. He told me about being confronted by a representative of the NRA when he was on the job. Everyone in the meeting at the DNR got quiet, he said.

The woods passed alongside us, as we ascended the hill. Tracks of squirrels or rabbits were in the snow below us. A ski pole lay in the snow where a skier dropped it accidentally.

Soon, we were at the top. The lift operator, whose job was to watch for skiers not getting off the lift safely, looked at us from his perch behind the window of the lift tower. We skied down the little hill by the lift and made the first turn of the day.

"To the right!" my brother yelled, and we warmed up on a run that took us to the tables by the chalet. This was our ritual, too, since we skied

Welch Village many times. Like riding a bicycle, my ski technique came back, like I did it yesterday. It was, in fact, my first time skiing this year.

I started with snowplow turns just to get the hang of my skis, then began stem Christies that took me into the fall line of the hill. Then I started parallel turns that drove me across the hill, in long traverses, arcing turns into the next traverse, then a series of tight turns that ended at the bottom of the run. A straight schuss on the flats led to the lift shed, where my brother, who was ahead of me, and I boarded the lift for the next run.

The operator said hello and held the chair under us. It swung around on the wheel powerful enough to run the entire lift and a hundred people on it up and down a ski hill all day. Once again, the chair oscillated back and forth toward the towers that supported it then settled. The woods passed us.

Mozart's horn concertos played in my ski helmet and we swung our skis like scissors beneath us. I was amazed how it all came back, since I skied so little these days. There was no protective bar in front of us to keep us from falling from the chair, but we felt secure anyway. It was a long drop to the ground.

We skied this run several times to get our ski legs, warmed up, and used to the snow conditions, which were spring like. The sky was clear, it promised to be a warm day, and the day before this was warm, too. This caused icy conditions when the snow thawed, froze at night, and was groomed by Snow Cats early in the morning.

Right now, the conditions were wonderful, with corduroyed snow that was not a hill of ice marbles, but that would change as the day went on. By afternoon, the hills would be slushy, with "corn snow." This condition was caused by skiers making turns in wet snow that ground into kernels. It was spring skiing and, right now, we reveled in the groomed hills. Our skis rippled on the groomed snow. We skied behind the lift shed, on a run that let our skis go. We turned long, carving, accelerating turns that took us along an expanse of snow and over a lip to a steep that led to the lift shed of a chairlift that serviced the runs at the back of the area. It was a fun run, forgiving, and easily skied.

At the top, we took another run that was an expert run all the way down. It started gradually, then dropped in a pitch that did not relent, until it flattened into a gut busting level that led to the lift shed. I was tentative at first then got my rhythm and finished strong.

My brother was skiing well. He skied a lot in his retirement and his technique, always strong from the French technique we learned as boys on a family trip to Big Mountain, Montana, was pretty. He kept his skis together, too closely for the modern ski technique, but his position over them was good. He was blessed with good legs that ran in our family.

There were a few people in line and we got in line and boarded the lift. The operator listened to rock music on the radio and another operator shoveled snow onto the lift platform. The chair came quickly, and I almost fell out of it, because I was not prepared.

This time we ascended the ski hill itself. Below us were children, hardly bigger than their boots, skiing among the moguls that billowed alongside the run, next to the trees that bordered it. The children handled the moguls and negotiated them without missing a beat. Their skis weaved through the troughs of the bumps.

One skier schussed the hill, making long turns that made him go faster at each turn. He was a racer and skied fast and gracefully and drove his skis through each turn. His body stayed ahead of his skis and his poles directed his movements.

The hill extended below us, like a pitched field of snow. I listened to Mozart's *Don Giovanni*, my brother told me how his children were doing, and we decided to take one of the double black diamonds at the back of the area. These were hills so steep they made our hearts go into our throats just looking at them. We skated off the lift and my brother herringboned toward a precipice. We stopped at the top and looked down. Our skis stuck out over the edge. There was an oak tree that grew miraculously in the middle of the run.

My brother pushed off. Quickly, he hung on for dear life. I shoved off, turning tight turns that held the fall line. I knew, if I traversed the hill, I would end up in the woods and wrapped around a tree.

"Stay on them," I told myself, as I angulated into each turn then into the next. The run flattened abruptly at the bottom and shot us onto a cat track that traversed below the double black diamonds. We decided not to do it again.

Then we had lunch. We skied to the front of the area, kicked off our skis, and clumped up the stairs of the chalet to the second floor where we left our boot bags that morning. I got in line at the cafeteria and bought a bowl of wild rice soup. My brother brought a lunch of yogurt and a tangelo.

My brother and I fought for a place to sit down and eat. Young ski racers yelled and screamed around us. They were with their parents, well behaved, and kept track of their gloves, helmets, and goggles that lay on the tables. Where the money came from for a young family to pay for ski equipment, lift tickets, and lunch every weekend for even one child, let alone two or three, was beyond me.

I was so poor my sense of economics was skewed. These people were middle class or well to do. Even a used car was out of my price range. The economic issues these people lived with were foreign to me. I skied because I was raised to it. It was now a lifestyle out of my league.

Outside the window, the front hill looked like a ski area in Japan. There was a line at the lift of fifty people, the tables were crowded with people eating lunch, and the hill was populated with skiers weaving in and out of each other. Somehow, they did not collide.

We finished lunch and put on our helmets, goggles, and gloves. We clumped past the crowd, through the wooden door, and down the metal steps to our skis. We stepped into them and skated to the lift. This time the skating was easier.

We warmed up on the forgiving run then took a black diamond located to the side of the back area. It was steep, fell away inevitably, and my brother took it without fear. I was more hesitant, until I got the feel of the run, and finished in a series of long, sweeping turns to the lift shed.

The snow was heavy, now, and it took more effort to turn our skis. The hill was skied out in places, with too many skiers grinding the snow into ice. Corn snow formed in pockets on the run where skiers made frequent turns.

It was getting warmer. I began to sweat. My forehead was dripping sweat under my ski helmet. My long underwear was wet around my neck and under my armpits.

We skied the expert run we skied earlier to the saloon at its base. We took off our helmets and parkas and I bought coffee for both of us. Neon signs lit the interior of the bar and the sun poured in the window. The bar was noisy and warm, icicles melted down its windows, and people wore turtlenecks.

We sat on a bench out front and the sun burned our faces. Before I left the hi-rise, I put on sunscreen to protect myself from the skin cancer I was prone to. My face was pale from the stuff and my helmet had a residue of it on its brim.

People crowded around a pond of water that skiers crossed in bikinis or swimsuits, after schussing a hill that took them at speed across the pond. Men in scuba suits supervised them, as they fell in the pond and tried to extricate themselves from their skis. A few made it, but most fell in the water.

The crowd cheered whenever someone fell or made it across the pond. People hoisted beers or wine as the skiers came down the hill at top speed and shot across the water on the narrow surface of their skis. We could tell if someone was going to make it by the way they held their balance on the water. They got their boots wet, too.

We found our skis, in a complex of them, and skied to the front of the area. Once again, we rode the chairlift and felt the glare of the sun off the snow on our faces. The run below us was the forgiving run and one man skied it, out of control. I was amazed at how little training people needed to have fun on skis.

We moved to the front of the area and found a run that was challenging. It started on a flat that dropped inexorably to the bottom, without letting up for a moment. It was like skiing the front half of the world. If I got back on my skis, I was a goner. I hung on, driving short turns down the fall line, next to the trees.

The sun was lower, and the runs were beginning to ice up. It was difficult to see the terrain and some hills were in the shade. So, we decided to stay on the hill we started on. It was shaded, too, since the sun was setting behind it.

It was quitting time and we wanted to ski safely to enjoy the skiing tomorrow. We skied slowly, to avoid injury. A skier always got hurt on their last run.

Andy Roberts
Three Poems

Clean Down to the Bone

Corrupted by the honey and gravel of Mr. Armstrong,
the muted horn of Holiday, steeped
in the mystic of Morrison,
I absorb with thrill and delight the past.

What's old is best tonight.
Ray, Hoagy, Jimi, Ella
singing *Georgia*.......*Georgia*........
drummer with brushes, standup bass, vibes.

Miles Davis, Bill Evans, Mr. Peter Green,
Keef and Charlie deep in the groove.
James Brown on the one, Sly and Marvin,
Curtis Mayfield says *Freddie's Dead*.

Gutshot by blues,
loving all that
cool dirty rhythm
all the way down to the bone.

Success

I've gotten pretty good at
the ambiguous love letter.
It feels safe enough
on the keys.
It's boredom I'm defeating,
but the price is high.

There she is
on the front lawn at 2:00 a.m.,
bottle of wine and a faceful of tears.
"I don't know," I tell my wife.

"She's nuts."

"No, don't call the police.
"She'll go away."

I always wanted to be a writer.

American Beauty

She left the planet courtesy
of sixty klonopin, genetics,
wicked little pistol in her left hand
she never had to use.
Now she's gone and all you have
left is your love for her
sailor's mouth, dragstrip courage.
You play the Dead's "Ripple"
in a futile attempt to bring some
church to your misery.
Punish a bottle of Johnnie Walker Red
with your lips in a gesture of
drunkenness that never had a shot.
Resort to the Argentine Tango
with a mop. Toss the condo,
find only dead soldiers,
twelve Excedrin Extra Strength.
They go down bitter.
Why couldn't we go out together,
your last cogent thought,
hand in hand, flat on our backs
here on the floor with
American Beauty spinning
till the needle digs a hole through?

Tomer Klein
Three Poems

A Bird of Prey

You swooped down on me
a kite on its prey
your claws are sharp and comforting,
your kisses are etching and caressing.

Your touch is night's forgetfulness,
for me your breath is like a prayer

Let's escape
into the depth of the moment

Savanna

A herd of words paced in tranquility
in the memory savanna
between synapses of Baobab trees
their roots raging
through a rugged heart.

A herd of words,
scorched by thirst,
parked by the lake of inspiration,
gulped liquid thoughts exuberantly,
rare drops of a Muse,
in the wilderness of Creation's desert

A herd of words aligned in a sentence,
its iambic legs paced steadily, rhythmically,
the structure and motif marked
the blank page.
A myriad of **dancing** colors
in a parade.

Centigrade 232

It was delightful
to burn moments
like elusive shreds of paper
fluttering upwards.

I sealed the time
or the
beginning of its recreation
with a blue flame
and departed
with a silent cry

Dave Hunter
Ronnie

When I heard that he had killed a young woman, I was not surprised. And though I had never heard of her, still I was sure he'd destroyed something of far more value than himself. I am not one of the pious who announce there is nothing more precious than human life. They say that it's scarcity that makes gold, diamonds, and managerial talent valuable. Then wolverines and black footed ferrets are more precious.

Ronnie was twenty-eight. I didn't know that until I read it in the paper.

In some ways, like not having any common sense, or worries, he seemed younger, like a teenager. But in other ways he seemed older. Like a throwback to when they made the movie that spawned the tv series, Happy Days, when cars had six or eight cylinders and if you lifted the hood you could see the wires running from the distributer to the plugs and the air filter sitting over the carburetor and it all made sense.

I guess I should make it clear that Ronnie didn't hunt this woman down and stab or shoot or strangle or beat her with the blunt object. No, he ran into her with his car as he was speeding through a residential area and she stepped out of her vehicle, I guess without looking both ways, and pow, she and her car door went sailing. So this was an accident, and he didn't mean to kill her, and he'd never been in trouble before, and no one came into court and said, "but Ronnie's a worthless piece of shit who's always been careless of the lives of others." And, that's a thing I've never understood. If you set out to kill someone with good reason, why that's the worst thing you can do. I don't understand that. Like those idiot deer hunters who shoot at sounds and kill six or seven other hunters every season; I think they should get life. I'd rather have killers that are looking for a certain someone, perhaps with good reason, because they're not going to get me. But these careless, sloppy, bastards might.

The neighbors who came out when they heard the crash said that Ronnie was inspecting the front end of his car with the young woman's body crumpled in the street ahead. Might be true, might not, people like to make things sound worse than they already are. With the help of a public defender, Ronnie pled guilty to negligent homicide, bargained down, I suppose, from who knows what. And, according to the ten o'clock news, a big deal was made of the fact that he had no alcohol in his blood at the time of the accident. I don't know what that had to do with anything. How much stupid did he have in his system? Anyhow, he got ten years.

Of course, he didn't do ten years. He did three years. Out on parole early for good behavior and because the prison was filling up with people who had sold drugs to people who wanted them.

When Ronnie went away he was a scrawny drink of water, but when he came back, he had muscles in his ear lobes. Three years of lifting weights at taxpayer expense. And I gotta bitch about that. Not so much in Ronnie's case, but I'm thinking of Obbie Nelson who was also a skinny punk when he held up the Get n Go, but he came back a muscular thug who broke Tom Robbin's jaw with a single punch. I don't want the state making these bastards more dangerous than when it got them.

After the trial, Ronnie's mother paid to have the car he loved, his red and white '65 Barracuda, towed from the cop's storage area to Hal's Storage, which is kitty corner from my home. And Hal Stover put the car way down in the corner of his fence, directly across from my front porch. I knew it was Ronnie's car and that it was a Plymouth Barracuda because Hal told me. He stops over for a beer now and then when he has some work to do at his storage place. Which is not all the time, because Hal didn't invest in this business so he could work eight to five. Mostly he's there because someone hasn't paid the storage fee for two months and he's emptying out that unit and sorting the remains for auction.

I wondered why the vehicle was setting out in plain sight and not inside one of the units. "It's seventy-five dollars a month to store a car and that punk's mother can't afford that. Christ, Midtown charged her a hundred and fifty just to tow the car to my place. If she'd called me, I'd have driven it here for nothing. It can sit there for nothing. But I'm not putting it up on blocks for nothing. I told her to write or call her son and get someone to put it up on blocks and fill the cylinders with oil. I don't know if she did, but no one's shown up to do it. I ain't doing it, not for free."

I don't guess Hal sounded so tough when Ronnie showed up with his new muscles and mad. Mad because the window of his precious killer car had been smashed and the tires had all gone flat, and there were small boxelder trees growing on the front seat.

"Damn! I store his goddamn car for free for three years, and does he thank me? Fuck no! He thinks it's my fault. And he wants to see the film from the security cameras. And when I tell him they're dummies, he's really pissed. Fuck him. I told him to get his fucking car out of my property or I'd sell it for scrap."

Well, that wasn't exactly how Ronnie told it to me. I suppose Ronnie had calmed down some since he'd talked to Hal. I imagine a guy learns how to calm down in the joint. Ronnie came to see me after going to Hal's Storage. Ronnie wanted to know if I'd happened to see who'd thrown the cement block through his window, or if I'd heard any rumors in the neighborhood about who might have done it. I told him I didn't, and I must have been downtown when it happened or I would have heard it, but I didn't.

He said, "You know for three years all I've thought about was getting that chine running again. It really hurt to see her all busted up. Fortunately, Mr. Halverson said I could keep it there for free until I can get it repaired. It's gonna take more than I expected. I suppose it was family or friends of that girl that jumped out in front of me. Well, let me know if you happen to hear anything."

I said I would, but I lied. I lied on two counts, because I knew who threw the rock that shattered the windshield into spider webbing and then the cement block that went through it. Because I watched him do it.

I was Danny Robinson. Danny's a big sixteen-year old high school dropout, though he didn't go much before he was a dropout. And Danny seemed to be some kind of natural leader, because he'd gathered a close cadre of five guys and probably another four hangers-on, or outriders. You know what they say: when you see dogs or teenagers running in packs you can bet they're up to no good. So far as I know, smashing the window of the Barracuda was the worst they'd done. But I hate to see it get started, because this sort of thing tends to escalate. So far Danny was the only one to quit school, but I didn't think it would be long before some of his buddies decided to join him, and then we'll have a group of unemployed teens with time on their hands. I know they smoke some pot and drink a bit of booze, because I can smell it on them when they come over. Oh yes, they come over in the evening. I've heard them say up the street, because my hearing is still really good, better than my eyes, "Let's go listen to Old Man Hunter bitch." That's okay. I'd just as soon stay on a speaking basis with them, especially if they turn to the real bad.

Fimicolous, that's a new word to me. I ran into it in a book on mushrooms. It means raised in shit and it describes most of the kids out in the northeast corner of town. I know in most towns it's East Side, or East End, or South Side, or the bottoms, or the wrong side of the tracks, but in our town it's the northeast corner and the tracks run right through it, not on one side or the other. I don't think there's a kid in Danny's group that's got a complete set of parents. This is the corner of town that gets more than its fair share of welfare checks, food stamps, and child support checks, and subsidized housing. This is the land of the single mother. Except they aren't really single. They're home watching soaps with their motorcycle moron boyfriends while their offspring roam the neighborhood unsupervised. And they love them, yes they do, they've bawled it out with the crumpled kid in their arms when the kid gets hit by a car or the train. But it's a sentimental love, like you have for a puppy. They don't love them enough to do the hard stuff like teaching the kids enough manners or morals, so they don't grow up to be a pain in the ass to everyone else. And a lot of them are kids themselves, the moms I mean. But what are you going to do?

So one fine evening after Ronnie's visit I'm sitting out on my porch and mellowing into the evening, as I was the night I saw Danny smash the windshield. I don't know if he or his posse saw me. There's a street light on the corner, one of the town's last, where the car was, and I was in the dark. There was a rock, a milky quartz, about the size on an acorn squash in the grass by the corner that I'd thought about bringing home because it was pretty. But then why bring it home when I could enjoy it right where it was? That was the rock Danny picked up and pitched over the fence. It splintered the windshield and bounced onto the hood. Danny and his boys vanished for maybe twenty minutes and then he came back with a cement block from I don't know where, and it did go through. I guess I should give him credit for persistence.

Okay, as I started to say, I'm out on the porch mellowing into the night when Danny and a couple of his pals stop by. "How's it going old man?" That's his usual greeting.

"Not bad young punk," that's mine. He and his pals laugh, I don't.

"By the way," I tell him, "Ronnie Withers is out of prison."

"Who the fuck is Ronnie Withers?"

"He's the proud owner of that car sitting over there with the busted window."

"That old wreck?"

"Weird as it seems, he loved that old wreck."

"Ain't none of my business. Anyhow, what was he in prison for?"

I could have been more exact, but I didn't want to be. "He killed someone."

Danny looked startled, but he recovered. "Well, I gotta be moving along. Can't be wasting my time with an old porch monkey." He and his pals headed out away from the light toward the abandoned cement factory.

I'm not trying to make friends with the boys, but I don't mind talking to them. Why not? And I figure if they ever really turn to the bad, it might cut me a little slack. I've never invited them into my house, and I don't plan to. They aren't my friends. Someday they might be fellow citizens, if we're lucky. There was an old fellow not too long ago in this town, but not in this neighborhood, who tried making friends with, what do the do-gooders call them? Kids at risk. I think he was lonesome. He was a coin collector and he showed the boys his collections. They killed him for his coins. And they were so goddamn stupid they were spending the coins for face value.

Some of Ronnie's story I can tell because it happened right in front of me, but other parts I heard from others, and I'm sure I didn't get everything. Someone told me that Ronnie had gotten a job on a roofing crew. So I'd say he was still being punished, because I think I'd rather sit in jail than work on a roofing crew, which is pretty close to being in hell. I heard he was still questioning people in the area about who might have pitched the concrete block, and he was convinced it wasn't a relative of the of the dead girl, because she didn't have any brothers or cousins, only two old parents, and Ronnie didn't think her friends would venture into this part of town at night. It was that "might have" part of the question that I figured might eventually lead him to Danny. If someone were to ask me who I thought "might have" lit up the old dried X-mas trees, broke the windows in the abandoned house, or lain a steel rod across the tracks by the crossing, and I were in the mood to make a guess, I'd probably come up with Danny, and I'm sure I'm not the only one who would.

Another summer night and I've settled into my chair, which is not some uncomfortable wooden piece of crap, but a nice rocker recliner, because I spend most evenings out here, what with the crap on tv, and since the city started spraying the damn skeeters, which I have to say is one fine thing, and I hope it's not killing the birds, but if it's shortening my life by a couple years I don't mind, I'd trade a couple years, especially at the end, for skeeter free evenings. And I noticed right off there's a rectangle of dead weeds where the red and white Barracuda used to be and I guess that means Ronnie came and put tires on it and had it towed to his mother's. About 8:30 the corner street lamp came on and Danny and just a couple of his boys turned up. I've got a big granite rock and one leg of a split rail fence in my front yard that came with the house. Danny and his pals perched on the rock and the fence like a troupe of vultures. They were passing a joint back and forth, something they'd never done right in front of me. I wasn't sure what it meant, if anything, or what I thought of it. Because I don't like sneakiness and if you're not ashamed of what you're doing, why hide it? On the other hand, it was still illegal, and I didn't think this was a Gandhi or Martin Luther King type of civil disobedience. But it wasn't my problem.

"You want a hit, Old Man?"

"I'll pass."

"What're you scared?"

"I wouldn't want to see you boys arrested for contributing to the delinquency of a senior."

They got a chuckle out of that. There was some other chatter that is lost, but I clearly recall Ronnie boiling out from somewhere beside my house, which I didn't like, and I still don't like the idea of anyone skulking around my house in the dark, but that's sort of beside the point, then and now. He came rushing out looking really big and muscular in a white tar streaked tee shirt, and he grabbed Danny by the neck with one hand and said mean and low like Clint Eastwood, "You're the punk that mashed my windshield."

"Wasn't me," Danny croaked.

Whack. Ronnie backhanded him. "Don't lie to me. Don't ever lie to me." And he slapped him again for emphasis. "I'm gonna tell you how it's gonna be. After school, in the evenings when you're out of school and I'm off work, you're gonna help me get my 'Cuda back to original condition."

I'll give Danny some credit, he looked like he was going to cry right in front of his pals, but he held back like a man and said, "I don't go to school."

"You think I don't know that? But you're going to. School starts in a week and you're gonna be back in it, or else you're going to be up on the roof with me and paying me back in cash. And if I hear you're not back in school and you're not roofing with me, I'm gonna hunt you down and kick your ass. Got it?"

And that's how it went down. Really. Danny and Ronnie tore out and replaced the upholstery and the windshield and put on four new tires and the death machine is running again with Danny riding shotgun and Ronnie teaching him to drive so he can get his license. And, Danny's in school and passing, so I hear, and Ronnie checks up on him and looks at his report card and pats him on the back when he does well. And I'm glad, because all his buddies didn't drop out, which I think they would have if Danny had stayed out, so I don't have a pack of worthless teens hanging around the neighborhood.

Oh yes, this is something I forgot to tell you, but when Ronnie was holding him by the neck and telling him how it was going to be, Danny asked, "Did he tell you?" meaning me. And Ronnie said, "He could have, but he didn't. He's old, he's from back when people didn't tattle." And that was kind of nice, though I'm not that damn old.

Okay. But before you go getting a lump in your throat at this tale of redemption and assumption of responsibility, remember there's a dead young woman at the back of it who just got out of her car at the wrong moment.

David Carkhuff
Homeless in Vacationland

Hey, you! You, in the tent!" The words jarred me awake. Rain pounded on the tent roof. I shook off my drowsiness and cried back, "Yeah?" "Monica has been trying to reach you. You need to call her. She said it's an emergency." The campground attendant buzzed away on his four-wheeler, while I searched for my TracFone. I found it and discovered the volume was turned down. Great. I was homeless in the back woods of Maine, and my one means of communication, a pay-as-you-go cell phone, had been silenced. Monica sobbed when I reached her. "I thought you had killed yourself," she said. "I really thought from the way you were acting last night, you meant to hurt yourself." Monica, like me, was homeless. She was living out of her SUV with everything she owned packed into her vehicle. Her therapy dog, Kiya, a black pug, had to be dropped off with friends. They owned a single-wide occupied by several dogs and cats, but out of the kindness of their hearts, they had taken in Kiya and stored a few of Monica's more important possessions. Monica had no choice but to leave Kiya there. The humidity and temperatures in Maine both had crested to unbearable levels.

How had we reached this point? Only a year and a half earlier, I had worked full time, part of a 25-year career in journalism, and I had enjoyed a comfortable yearly salary of over $40,000. It seemed like a dream.

Monica and I lived for a time in a mobile home in Brunswick, Maine, a bedroom community less than a half hour north of Portland. We enjoyed our pug, Kiya, and traveled around Southern Maine, almost like tourists, even though Monica had grown up and lived her life in Central Maine. But Maine is expensive, and relationships are hard. We sold the mobile home, and in a state of some disarray, we found rooms at a motel near Portland where Monica had spent years working at the front desk. I tried to carry on with my journalism career while tending to our marriage. But the start-up newspaper that had been the lure to bring me out to Maine, and which had resulted in me meeting Monica, faltered under the pressures on print media. The paper folded. My boss transferred me to an alternative weekly which he had purchased. Turmoil ensued. When I transferred again to work as a reporter at a traditional daily in New Hampshire, the move took a further toll on our marriage, as Monica stayed to work at the motel near Portland. I had chosen work over Monica and our marriage. Then came cancer. Monica received the breast cancer diagnosis while I was covering town meetings. We both were stunned. I drove the two-hour back-roads trip to Maine on weekends to be with her, while trying to maintain my reporting job. Finally, I talked with my boss. He told me I could have a week off. After 11 years. I quit.

So there we were, in a Maine motel, me working the front desk (a job I had never done) and doing housekeeping. Monica prepared for her surgery, receiving assurances that the medical system would carry her through with its myriad support services and ample after-care. None of that proved to be remotely accurate. Monica underwent the reduction and reconstruction surgery to rid her of the cancer. But in the aftermath, we were abandoned, left to struggle with no instructions and the wrong types of bandages and bras. The nurse navigator was nowhere to be found. Monica contracted MRSA and nearly died from this persistent infection. When a Portland hospital admitted her to administer antibiotics, they dumped her in the dialysis wing, with only a dirty curtain separating her from a coughing and hacking patient. And she tried to cover her open wounds while suffering abuse from the nursing staff. A surgeon finally signed off, and we walked out in the middle of the night. Then came the ordeal with caring for a neglected grandson. Monica's son seemed incapable of taking responsibility for his son, a sensitive and smart little boy born in the same Portland hospital where we had experienced such shoddy care. Adam lived an itinerant life, shuffling from apartment to apartment, in what we called flophouses. Someone flung mattresses on the floor, and the children piled onto them. Dirty and clean clothes lay in piles. The mother worked and expected relatives or past partners to care for three boys, including Adam, the most recent addition. We took Adam under our wing because nobody else would. We now lived in a cramped, third-floor attic apartment in Waterville, back in the Central Maine town where Monica had spent so much of her life. Even as poorly equipped as we were, we agreed that without our help, Adam might suffer the type of scarring abuse that would damage him for life. We already knew about rampant neglect, where he was left unattended for hours at a time. So we took him in. Another long saga would end in heartbreak. A generous group of caregivers, mostly grandparents who had adopted troubled grandchildren, helped us initially with food, clothing, and even a makeshift metal bunkbed. Adam improved in school, receiving attention he had never before enjoyed. We took him to parent-teacher conferences. The mother drifted along with us, barely interested but giving us enough permission to continue. Then, we caught Adam trying to sexually abuse another child. That was the end. We had no choice but to send him back. Clearly, Adam had been abused, and now he was poised to continue the cycle. He was placed in counseling in a new town and new school system. Monica sobbed over the loss of a beloved grandson, but she couldn't condone his behavior, and we were not in a position to help him on that level. And then came the notification from my family. We were still reeling from the Adam episode when I learned that my mother was confined to a nursing home, and the cost threatened to deplete the family's resources. My brother, Ian, described a bleak situation where

Mom could come home, but only if someone could stay up at night and help her hobble into the bathroom. Mom had broken a hip and had begun experiencing dementia. Ian had a full-time job and had exhausted himself caring for Mom. So, in the worst decision of my life, I dropped everything, left Monica alone in that attic apartment with reminders of Adam everywhere, and I drove pell-mell across the country, sleeping in my car, and completed the 3,000-mile trip in four days. But I had to take care of my mother, and the nursing home was discharging her. Monica encouraged me. It was my mom, I couldn't just ignore the situation, she said. She had a special feeling for her mother, despite a complicated and difficult past. It was a tearful parting. The idea was that I would go out, size up the situation, and if it seemed necessary, return to pack up our belongings and bring Monica to stay with me while we lived on my parents' property in Idaho and looked after my mom. Monica had a long background in home care. She had suffered a debilitating back injury while working in the field. Yet, she was eager to stay with my mom and look after her. I had to clear up a few financial issues, and in lieu of a salary for living with my parents and staying up nights for Mom, I received help with car payments and a few other costs. I figured that if Mom were in a nursing home, the family would face costs of $5,000 a month, hardly a sustainable amount. But it was summer, and while the weather in Idaho was pristine, back in Maine, the heat and humidity were soaring. Monica and I had endured a frigid winter in the attic apartment. I naively assumed that the same conditions that had produced such cold surroundings in the cramped space—a faulty heating system and poor insulation—would somehow compensate in the summer and create a cool haven. That was a foolish pipe dream. The apartment was an oven, and Monica and Kiya suffered for it. Finally, I asked my father, and he agreed to pay for an air conditioner for Monica and Kiya. But this experience showed me the lay of the land financially. Ian and his partner exercised control over the parents' finances, even though they technically lacked a power of attorney or other legal mechanism to delineate the responsibility. But they were gracious about transferring funds when needed to help with my expenses. Until the bills mounted. Monica and I readied for a move from Maine to Idaho. She received my assurances that my family would pay her a stipend when she arrived and would arrange for some kind of living space. I flailed around looking first for a cheap apartment in Idaho and then for a cheap camper that could be our home on the property. We didn't want to crowd in on our parents. Though they lived on a dozen acres in the country, the house was a traditional layout, without any easy ground-level extensions for a couple to move into and tend to an 89-year-old mother who was stranded on the first floor. With my family's support, I flew back to Maine. My oldest brother, Carl, donated to the effort, even though he voiced frustration that my parents didn't just pay me directly and in an ample amount to manage a complicated, cross-country move. The same question echoed in my head. Why was I trying to vacate an apartment, equip an SUV for a 3,000-mile trip, and handle a thousand loose ends, including Monica's medical care for the pain inflicted by fibromyalgia, with only a few hints that everything would be all right? Our unease grew when I arrived and Monica realized that I didn't have a family credit card, perhaps one borrowed with permission from my father, to make sure we could handle unforeseen emergencies in our trip. When I inquired, Ian and his partner, Kris, who had taken on the role of de facto bookkeeper, replied that we could call and receive help if we needed an extra night in a motel or some other extremity. To further muddle the picture, the family recently had rearranged my parents' finances. In a move that created a mixed message, Ian even had loaned $8,000 of my father's money to a neighbor who handled some maintenance on the property. The reason was to prevent my father from earning too much income and scuttling an arrangement for state funding for my mother. My naivete again reared its head. I assumed that we could enjoy a win-win of sorts by counting on financial help from my parents that in turn would ease the concerns about Dad's income running afoul of the state regulations. Karl kicked in $1,000 and my parents, via Ian and Kris, contributed another $900 to give us some footing once I arrived in Maine. But Monica saw the warning flags. We needed to stay in a cheap motel – one where the managers rifled through our belongings when we were gone and pestered Kiya, but that's another story for another time. So we holed up a few miles out of Waterville and finished emptying the apartment. Monica never wanted to set foot back in that attic prison. She had fallen several times on the steep stairs. The place was now a shell. We looked forward to returning the keys and bidding farewell. But now Ian was sounding some alarms. He wanted to know when we would be arriving so he could get back to living his life and stop staying up with Mom and looking after her before and after work in the daytime. Yet at the same time, when Monica tried to have a conversation with him about a stipend, Ian evaded the question. He said he had a wine and painting party underway on the property and needed to return to his guests. The timing couldn't have been worse. Monica balked. She sensed that the family's true intention was to lure her out to Idaho and keep her there looking after our mother without a financial plan in place to make sure she could tend to her needs. Now, I had to break the news to Ian and Kris that we weren't coming. Through the entire miscommunication and misunderstanding, Monica was now homeless. She was furious with me, and understandably so. My position wasn't much better. I was homeless with her. We couldn't go back to the apartment. We didn't have any intention of paying August's rent, and anyway, the landlady was under the impression that we were moving out. We had less than $2,600 to live on, counting a check I had received for copywriting. But my income was only based on part-time writing for some friends who ran a communications business. And the money began to dwindle.

Ian grew confrontational, even as we faced our crisis. He wondered if the pattern of spending that we had exhibited pointed to a drug habit. This suggestion was laughable, as Monica cringed at taking even the legal medications that eased the persistent pain from her surgery. I scarcely even touched alcohol, although I was reconsidering as the stress mounted. Then, Ian informed me that several of his friends suggested that they press charges and have us arrested for misuse of my parents' funds. This accusation rang a bit hollow considering that Ian and Kris had lived for years rent free on my parents' property, and that they were now controlling my parents' money in a legally dubious manner. But we were now on the horns of a dilemma. Monica hated me, and we fought because of the ordeal that I had helped inflict. Her family despised me. We packed everything she owned into totes and bags and crammed them into her SUV. It became clear that I would need to give away what remained of my belongings. We stayed at another cheap motel, but only for a night, as we realized that the money situation was perilous. Now, I pleaded with my brothers to give me one last financial assist. The logic on our end made sense. Through their negligence, they had left Monica homeless and with no way to live. She now was glad she had not given up on applying for affordable housing in Maine. But that process would not happen overnight. We faced two months or more of waiting. It wasn't even clear I could come with her. Our relationship had taken one too many body blows. My presence and even my meager income would only complicate her attempts to get into housing. So we took our camping gear, purchased in a much happier time in anticipation of traveling across the country to help my mom, and we paid $40 for a campsite in the woods about 15 miles outside of Waterville. The ironies ran deep. Monica had shopped like a pro, saving my parents money through her frugal and intense efforts. The whole point of buying a tent and related equipment was to avoid the costs of motels when we traveled to Idaho. Now, we used the gear for a different reason. We had no home and needed to conserve what was left of our dwindling funds. But the pristine lakeside campground occupied by happy families only deepened our grief. On one night, Monica told me she could no longer bear being without Kiya, her therapy dog and best friend. So near midnight, she dropped me off at the campground in the pouring rain and told me she would come back in a couple of days when we needed to check out. Where we would go then was unclear. By this point, I could no longer react. My brother, Ian, rebuffed any requests for emergency help, instead accusing me of misusing the money we had received. In a stroke of cruel twistedness, a promise of $1,000 from Carl to salvage our situation and begin making amends with Monica was withdrawn. Kris had talked to Carl. Somewhere a mind was changed. That money would be directed toward a month of overnight care for Mom. That way, Ian could continue with his life and participate in a series of reunion concerts with a rock band he had joined earlier in life. Kris could even join him at one of the concerts. Essentially, we would live homeless so my brother and his partner could carry on with their social lives instead of caring for Mom, which seemed to be the duty they had assumed by living off my parents for all those years. And when my mother called me to ask what was going on, she and Dad agreed they were willing to help us. But in the infuriating situation, because of their declining health, I could only filter the request through their money managers, Ian and Kris. My request at this point was for a $500 check sent directly to our landlady. We would reverse gears and beg to be let back into the attic apartment. But even this request was refused. Ian and Kris wanted us out there in Idaho to relieve their burden. Never mind that we now had no practical way of traveling cross-country. They viewed life only through their own prism of needs and wants and a somewhat pampered lifestyle where they could work their jobs but live without worry about rent or food. Monica was having none of it. They would not blackmail or coerce us. She would rather live homeless, out of her SUV, then buckle to their wishes and grovel for whatever money they would dole out. Communications between Monica and

my brother, always tentative, ended. I maintained only a frail connection with both of my brothers. Clearly, they all felt exhausted and frustrated. Meanwhile, I was trudging through the rain, in the dark, prepared to spend a night in a tent while the love of my life wondered if I was contemplating suicide.

The lesson from this entire experience is simple. Even the best intentions can't replace common sense. Don't try to help others if you will end up crippling yourself and the ones you love. My mom will receive care, even though the manner in which it has been planned and carried out could be called shoddy at best. Monica and I found that the experience of losing our physical possessions and certainty about where we would live deepened our feelings for each other. The ordeal, although emotionally draining and physically exhausting, gave use a new perspective on what counts in life. Meanwhile, my hope is that anyone who goes about their daily existence and notices one of those homeless people on a street median or sidewalk will exercise some compassion. Nobody is immune to the vagaries of life and the pull of emotion over reason. We learned this lesson the hard way.

Dan Butterfass
Nametag *Peggy*

Where she came from
You'll never know
Other than it was a hard
Long road to the back

Of the convenience
Store service counter
Where she always
Greets you smiling

Sincere and bug-eyed
Lids shadowed turquoise
Thick as a child's mashed
Streaks of sidewalk chalk

Her voice like gravel
Scraping bottom
Of a whiskey barrel
Hello Dear

How are you today
Through neon lipstick
And stained mouthful
Of capped teeth

As you give something
Like alms for a cup
Of stale coffee
Or lottery ticket

For the chance
To conjure her former
Life as a gypsy
Fortune teller

Bead artist
Crash pad
Hippie strung out
At Haight-Ashbury

Someone told me
There's a girl out there
With love in her eyes
And flowers in her hair

Oversized lavender daisy
Hairclip still blossoming
From her wild frizzed
Cascade of greyed

Locks dyed half pink
Like Janis' if she'd kicked
Smack to ramble
On as long as Peggy

Whose identical tattoo
A Florentine bracelet
That waif personally
Drew out on her wrist

Backstage at Monterey
After tripping together
Slow-kissing in between
Swigs of Southern Comfort

Dancing front & center
In bell bottoms onstage
With Grace Slick at muddy
Peace soaked Woodstock

Areolas rippling through
A loose white blouse entranced
By Altamont's strange dream
Killing vibe of wickedness

Aboard the last hurrah
Of Festival Express' non
Stop jam sessions & all
Night partying with Jerry

Garcia's cock in her ass
A special kind of fame

Like her best friend
The Butter Queen
Stratospheric names
The Internet drops
Like acid on the tip
Of her tongue's

Photographic
Memory of sucking
Her generation's
Pantheon of genius

Dionysian energy
Of their minds
That launched her
Into rarefied orbit

Paramour goddess
Groupie girlfriend
Unpaid porn star
Nihilistic muse

Tangerine, tangerine
Living reflection from a dream
I was her love
She was my queen

Hearing the first riffs
Holding the notebook's
Lyrics she inspired
Played on the radio

Decades after
The party ended
With too many shared
Needles and friends

Dead by overdose
By suicide her own
Womb suffocated
By a growing

Family of abortions
Save for the last

Girl she refused
To kill and carried
Father unknown
From a cheap motel
Into an anonymous
Penniless gut

Wrenching adoption
That fed her
Tramped out
Chain smoking

Soul to a summer
Fair circuit's band
Of misfit carnies
Tilt-a-Whirl's

Kaleidoscopic
Midway hustle
For a decade
Long angry fix

In depraved
Trailer camp
Orgies with midgets
Writhing squished

To grotesque fatness
In the hermaphrodite's
Sick joke of fun
House mirrors

That shattered
Into a million
Little shards
Inside her

As she stared
Into an apparition
Of pure innocence
Laughing aboard

The miniature
Choo-choo

That transfigured
Into a graffitied
Boxcar trundling
Her down the rails
To nowhere in rat
Piss shaking DTs

To be on your own
A complete unknown
Like a rolling stone
No direction home

But for an uncanny
Notion she'd find her
Someday somewhere
As long as she kept

That blind faith
Walking the line
With her collar
Turned up

To a cold mean
Lonely wind blowing
Through all the nights
Since her rebirth

Transfixed by
The face of an angel
Somehow spared
AIDS grim specter

Like a curse lifted
Into her anonymous
Second life finding
Solace in ordinary

Steady work
As shift manager
Sometimes surprised
By her own grand

Motherly face

In the breakroom
Mirror held up
To a northern Podunk
She doesn't love
Or hate when
Its rivers freeze
And summer ends

With the snowflake
Storm through her
Trailer court window
As she sifts through

Unpublished Polaroids
Jim's buried in Paris
Mick still a fountain
Of leaping youth

Robert silent yet Jimmy
Facetimes once a year
Hey Merry Christmas
Fingering new chords

That always summon
Enough courage
To retry a tentative
Hand at writing

Her memories
By candlelight
Meteor showers
Outside her trailer

We are stardust
We are golden
And we've got to get ourselves
Back to the garden

Where she tends
A self-tilled patch
With hummingbirds
Buzzing her hibiscus

Neale Torgrimson
Department of Catastrophe Management

1.

Somewhere in the Department of Catastrophe Management is a photo of former FBI Director J. Edgar Hoover, his confidant Agent Clyde Tolson, and Liberace, the flamboyant entertainer. Rumors said it was in the Secretary's top floor office, hanging on a nail hammered into the wood paneling that covered the walls. The building had only been built in '96, but they went cheap and took

what old discarded Watergate-era government decor the other departments were oh so willing to purge. The President has just got done balancing the budget and creating a whole new bureaucracy. This was expensive business. Any and all corners would be cut, no exceptions, even for the Director.

In stark black and white clarity, it was the three men standing for a photograph, hands on shoulders, smiles in variants. The two G-men in black suits flanked Liberace, who was draped in flowing white furs and embedded jewels that lost none of their luster in the transformation from real life to photocopy. They were aligned in order of progressive height. The shortest, J. Edgar, was on the left. His body language was stiff, insecure, and he forced a canned, reluctant smile for the photographer. His arms were at his side even as the man in the center seemed to flow into him spatially. He had a bit of a deer in the headlights look, a man caught unawares mid-mugshot who had enough presence of mind to put out a canned teeth-in-grid smile so as to save some sliver of fleeting dignity and grace.

Liberace exuded a natural assuredness and self confidence that made J. Edgar on his right, photo left, seem to shrink into his own skin. He was naturally taller by about three inches or so and one couldn't rule out the possibility that underneath the silks and the sequins and the robes were a pair of pumps or heels. For all the glittering of his diamonds and jewelry, he seemed not to pay any recognition to them. There was an "Oh? These?" look about him that indicated status and wasn't in any way false. There was a very real possibility that he didn't own a single article of clothing that was neither bejeweled or fashioned with some other polished metal or semi-precious stone. The enthusiasm in his smile was evident, but then so too was his reserve: there was a second gear of happiness in there, disengaged. Here was a man enjoying the moment, but who had an eye for the bigger picture.

The man at right was tall and slender, but well built, even in his advanced age. J. Edgar would call Clyde Tolson "Junior" and was known to treat "Junior" as his son, his ward, his protege, his partner, his alter ego, and his soul mate, sometimes all within an hour. Tolson's broad shoulders seemed to expand beyond even their natural width, unchained by the social burdens that had previously inhibited both body and mind equally. Stiff in back and confidence, he stood unbent, as if for the first time in his adult life, jack-legged and tall, past the measures of his body or the borders of the photograph. He had a beaming, cockeyed grin, the kind of exuberance displayed almost exclusively in young boys in Little League, and only by those who played on the winning team. His Windsor knot had been loosened a measure, no doubt in the midst of a night's delight, and, sweat dabbed and diluted, his normally well-mannered hair was scattered in drippy strands across his face.

There was a line written in the dark room editing process in militant all caps that said, SANDS CASINO, LAS VEGAS, NEVADA-1956. The frame had a sort of mock-gilded elegance, the kind that once housed a mass printed copy of some Dutch master before it was bought for a couple of bucks at some Silver Springs Goodwill. Glued onto the surface of the frame was the material of a plastic nameplate that sat perched on the hundreds of desks within the Department of Catastrophes and across the various other government buildings citywide. It was slightly askew and said in thin, government bold: THREE QUEENS.

Richards came up from behind with a paper cone cup of water and began to quietly sing an alternate take to "Three Kings."

We Three Queens of Government Are ...

"What? No second verse, Richards?"

"I'm just repeating what I've heard. I would have thought you old Agency boys would have been working on it, Herman," he said before taking a sip from the paper cup. "I get it though. You can't rush genius, can you? Oh, and he's wrong by the way about the Secretary's office. It doesn't have wood paneling. Mahogany desks, sprawling windows overlooking the Potomac, Italian leather on the chairs. Herman wouldn't know, he only gets to see a window to go to lunch and go to HR, let alone go all the way up to the Secretary's office."

A polite laugh was shared by the young and clean-shaven members of the table and when the laughter stopped a few nervously tidied their lunch trays and unused napkins. Herman gave a "Like I Give A Shit?" look as he smirked and stroked his graying beard.

"Richards is just butt-hurt an Agency man is running the Department and not someone from the Bureau."

"Butt-hurt? Interesting choice of words for a... for a ... what's the word I'm allowed to use these days?"

"Careful, Richards. *You* wouldn't want to go to HR *right* after lunch, would you? Don't you want to spread your breaks out? Get some form of natural light in the afternoon?"

"I got a UV lamp down there. Helps with the crazy spells. HR visits cut in half. Does wonders, but I've got to remember to rotate it. Get both sides. Like in a tanning bed? The right side of my face was burning so much, I thought I had a stroke or something. Anyway, you were telling the pups a story."

"Oh, the Liberace story? That's nothing. Don't worry. There's more where that came from. Just you wait until I tell you about Hoover wearing women's underwear, or what the Director and Agent Tolson called each other when nobody was listening."

"So, somebody was listening then?"

"Of course, there was somebody listening. There's always somebody listening. There's always somebody watching. You think that was an American taking the "Three Queens" photo at the Sands? He was a Russian! Or a Hungarian, rather, but same bloc. It was from a hacked communique that came from our man in Gorky. Did you guys have a man in Gorky? It's a reprint, of course, but our man in Gorky confirmed the photo's authenticity and existence. We in the Agency used to call that sort of thing a Helsinki Hustle."

"What's a Helsinki Hustle?" asked one of the new kids.

"Well, Edwards. A Helsinki Hustle is when you steal something from the Russians and use it against the Bureau. That little beauty got us back in the good graces of some Mick gangsters who were running guns to the IRA and all of a sudden … decided to change their clientele."

Richards crumpled the paper cup and dumped it on Edwards lunch tray before pulling over a spare chair from a neighboring table. The young pups stopped touching the remaining mashed potatoes and the little plastic sheaths that came with their straws and were now full on checking their nautical watches, most likely gifts for graduating from their esteemed, brick and ivy institutions.

"I suppose he's going to justify a half century of dumping some white powder on the corners of South-Central LA and the Bronx, all so some Banana Republic paramilitary could afford to buy a Stinger or two."

"Two? We were doing 2-for-1 swaps, kilos for rockets. Coke or Dope. 3-for-1 if they wanted training on the damned thing first."

The quip got a grin or smirk from a pup or two, but the others were cold as stone, like a merit student waiting to be sent into the Principal's office. The cafeteria was beginning to fill in as 11 turned to noon. The cafeteria workers took away the last remaining steam tray of scrambled eggs and brought in a fresh batch of Beef Stroganoff for the lunch rush. The weatherman said that the clouds were going to lift right around midday and that, for the first time in four days, there'd be some sunshine. But if anything, there were more storm clouds rolling in. Richard's shirt creases seemed to tighten and stiffen as his tone became less slacked.

"I suppose you're going to justify spending millions of taxpayer dollars on booby trap cigars or exploding toilet seats to nail Castro or Gaddafi while we turned over couch cushions to find enough money for a goddamn WitSec Program so we could put away Gotti."

"Watch your mouth amongst the Mormons," referring to the pups. "And there you go about the mob again. It's always the mob. Mob, mob, mob, black militants, mob."

"We could have gotten him in an orange jumper 10 years earlier if it wasn't for you greedy Agency hogs."

"Sue me. We spent what we were given. Call your Senator, Richards."

There was a lull, a natural end point. They understood each other, or so it seemed. Herman was sitting back, but he had stopped being comfortable at that point and it was clear that he had had his fill. Richards was steely eyed, but his heartbeat was down a tick or two from when he crumpled up the cup. The pups finally began to breathe easy and circulate blood back into their face. Adjacent tables were all but full and those in the far corners of the cafeteria began to fill. It was in this moment when Richards waded back into the swamp to get in the last word.

"I can forgive all that. I can. The manipulations, the insurgencies, the counter-insurgencies, the revolutions, the counter-revolutions, then there's the assassinations, the coups …"

"Don't forget the time we tested LSD on Whitey Bulger when he was in the Atlanta pen," quipped Herman, adjusting his seat as he said it.

"I can even deal with the snarky, unprofessional bullshit. That flip, devil may care, do whatever works attitude? I can put up with it. Seriously. I can deal with it. Maybe even learn to like it. I can deal with all that, if it actually WORKED."

The last word rattled across the room like a rattling fork. It coincided with a random lull in the natural hum of the cafeteria. Every stray gaze and glance was magnetized to the table. Richard's cuff was Birdseye Green Peas stiff and the little dimple on his stone-cut jaw seemed to throb and pulsate, emitting frequencies that were sub-optical, not so much seen, but felt. And now that he had gotten everyone's attention, Richards wasn't finished.

"But it doesn't work, does it? Not really. It works for a minute. You arm the Mujahideen, they kill 2 Russian soldiers for every 10 of their own and that's a win-win. You pop champagne, you do a little blow, and you pat yourself on the back for ending history. It's never the end. You need a process to manage it, *police* it, but there is no process. Only the result. It doesn't matter how you get there, so long as it ENDS the way you want it to. But it never ends. But it isn't the end. History, as it turns out, doesn't end. It can't end. The good guys become the bad guys, the bad guys become the good guys, and the enemy of my enemy is my friend kind of circle jerk continues ad infinitum. And we're all stuck here, running things your way. The Agency way. No process, no standards, no procedure, no methodology. Identity? Long-term goals? What are they? Burdens to the present objective. Today is the only day that matters. 'Hm? Let's see. Shall we arm these right-wing nationalists to fight off the religious cultists we armed to take down the Anarcho-communists we put in power to undermine the monarchy? Why not? Just win baby. Just win.'"

He was deliberate, pointed, but never so emotional to be off the mark, every dart hit its intended point. Herman tried to laugh away the criticism, tried to slip out of the break.

"And why are we here in this department, this consolidated megalith of an intelligence apparatus? Why aren't you in Langley anymore? How come I'm no longer at the Bureau? Because you let the Bojinka cells go."

The laughter fell from Herman's face as quickly as the blood left the faces of the pups, as quickly as the rain broke from the cloud line in sheets onto the yellow grass on the courtyard below, forcing smokers to turn heel, snuff their Virginia Slims on black leather boot heels and stiletto toe taps, and head inside, trading one storm for another.

"That's bullshit, Richards. No, that's bull."

"Share information with the FBI or foreign intelligence services? No, they'll just scare away all the fish. Right?"

"Enough. Stop it, Richards"

"No, you let them go. You were on them and you let them go. Why? So, you could get the big fish? Let the little ones nibble away. Why pull them in when the trophy Bass is just another hour away? They're not Bass, they're Piranhas."

"Stop it, Richards. I mean it."

"And when they blew those planes up over the Pacific, killing thousands, most of whom were Americans coming home, coming home, Herman, coming home to see their families and they died and they all got away. Got away, Herman. Got away. It wasn't even a suicide attack. They just set the bomb underneath the chair and got off at the first stop. Did you and your Agency get the result you were looking for? Did the country get the result it was looking for?"

For as pale as the pups were, Herman was red as Mars and fuming like a sewer vent. Trails of sweat leaked from his scalp and evaporated before even reaching his thick beard. Wordless, he reached for his spoon that had a four-shell clump of macaroni salad still on it and flung it at the old G-Man, hitting

him in the chest. Richards put his chin to his sternum and watched the mayonnaise and the peas and the shells ooze down the shingle-stiff ridge of his button down. He looked up to Herman with a cocked eye, his chin dimple shrinking in a black hole collapse, and grabbed a remaining strand of Beef Stroganoff noodle from one of the pups' plates and flung it at Herman, landing on his face with a plop lengthwise across his beard and his lips, across the span of his face.

Herman grabbed a cherry tomato and flung it at Richards, but he was able to parry it with quick reactions and a neighboring lunch tray, spilling silverware onto the table with a clatter. The tomato ricocheted off the lunch tray and into the eye socket of Edwards. She responded by grabbing two glasses of water with each hand and flinging the contents out sprinkler-style and onto everyone seated at the table and onto a few others seated nearby.

A man who got a glassful of water onto his untouched lunch slammed his palms onto the table and, in mock Belushi, yelled "Food fight!" across the cafeteria. He had a half-smirk on his face as his tense shoulders slacked and his feet lead him back to his empty seat, thinking he had de-escalated the situation, only to be met by a spray of Bavarian Cheese Soup. The grin soon faded into a facial rictus of suspended horror as he was pelted by successive waves of carrot sticks, cantaloupe rinds, apple cores, tea bags, raisin boxes, cottage cheese, outflows of boxed apple juice and whole milk, kombucha, cold rolls, Russian dressing, dried cranberries, croutons, Kosher dill pickles in both spear and slice form, Land O' Lakes butter tabs, and little Andes mints that were meant to cleanse the palate after lunch. He fell like the first man in through the breach and then the real firefight began. Richards and Herman hit the deck as the pups went at each other with shakers of salt and tubes of ketchup and mustard. Edwards took a plate of stroganoff to the ribcage and frisbee of sourdough toast to the brow. The contractor chefs went about undertaking more idle tasks behind the counter while avoiding errant salad boxes and granola bowls, all with a "Same Shit, Different Day" sort of exhaustive expression, heat tempered and permanently locked into their faces.

Bananas were peeled and the fruit portioned into ration-able munitions, the peels strewn about the floor like Claymores. Napkins were wadded up and dunked in room temperature black coffee, before being hurled in arcs like mortars upon the clamoring ranks. Attaché cases and portfolios were used as emergency shields. String cheese tubes were left in their plastic tubes and whipped like tomahawks at the closest available targets. Elevator doors opened, but no one came out, all occupants more than willing to take an extraneous trip to the lower parking garages rather than enter the fray. A soiled few managed to drag their sauce covered bodies into the lift as the prior occupants hugged walls in hopes of avoiding physical contact with the pigpen dirty elevator riders.

The fracas finally ended when a jet of brown mustard fell upon the last step of the main staircase before the entrance to the cafeteria and the last drop came within inches of smearing the bald dome of the Undersecretary who was in conversation with the Secretary himself. All was silent as the Secretary and the Undersecretary inspected themselves for any yellowish stains. It was then that the Secretary gazed out upon the chaos that had transpired in the cafeteria and looked down upon his shoes to find a singular dime-sized drop of brown mustard upon his just polished shoes of black leather.

2. Florence, Colorado.
She waved a badge on a lanyard to the guard at the desk.

DepCat.

The guard made a call. The guards halted the call mid convo. "And you?"

I shook my head.

DOD? NSA?

"I'm private sector"

"A contractor?"

I smirked and nodded. Close enough.

He continued to talk on the phone. Eventually, he put it down and the buzzer went off. A door opened and a man with superior credentials walked through to escort us to another screening center down the hall where we were searched again. It looked like something more makeshift than the one we were forced through when we first entered the facility. As if it had been set up in an unused room specifically for our arrival. They had been expecting us.

"I'm sorry for the inconvenience, but I hope you understand. We don't allow many visitors and he doesn't have many fans."

"We're not fans," she says.

He eyed our briefcases. They'd been scanned for the usual contraband. Still, he eyed it, but knew better than to ask. I took off my jacket in the search and there, in the breast pocket, they found the masks.

"What's this? You sure you need these? You know he ain't getting out, right? He's on a life sentence and he's got another 240 more years tacked onto that just in case he manages to make it out of this world alive."

"I'm a slave for appearances."

"Have it your way," he said

After the check, we made for his wing. We entered a tall antechamber that lead to multiple wings. All of them cathedrals of pain. His wing had been nicknamed Bomber's Row by the guards. It eventually got leaked to the papers and naturally stuck. Locked away in there were about a dozen religious zealots, red-wave internationalists, radical secessionists, white supremacists, militant crypto-fascists, and anarcho-primitivists. Their singular connection was the bomb, the science of making it and the art of using it. The odd duck was a Texas orderly at a mental institution who intentionally altered the dosages so that 14 medically infirmed patients would OD on their meds and die. And they did. He said that he didn't do it for ideology or money or anything. Just because. That's all. He wasn't a bomber, but, somehow, he seemed to fit right in.

Our escort updated us on the situation of the inmate. We were told of the conditions of his imprisonment. We were told of his rejection of Islam, of how he befriended a bomber of Federal buildings, of his subsequent conversion to Christianity, of how he began to eat pork and often spoke in tongues. We were told of the time he carved a crucifix into his forehead with a fork he was using to eat pork cutlets and how the wound had healed, but the scar remained. We were told of the subsequent fork ban and his forced diet of soft foods. We were told of his hunger strike and his refusal to eat until he was fed pork again. We were told of the genius of prison chefs who cut the pork into smaller bits and breaded them like nuggets and served them to him like that. We were told of the tremendous amount of weight he had put on and how the prison physician advised against his diet and thought it would put overt strain upon his organs and ligaments. We were told of his limited exercise due to the specific spatial constraints by his imprisonment. We were told that he lacks the sheer human will to do anything except pray and eat pork nuggets. We were told these things as if we didn't already know. It was all in the dossiers and they were already in the briefcases.

Two guards awaited us at his cell door up on the second flight of the second wing. Our guide motioned for them to open up the cell. Two thumps of the fist fall upon the sliding doors.

"Rise and shine, Porky Pig. You've got guests."

The doors slid mechanically open and the guards stood aside. Our guide motioned for us to proceed.

She said a little privacy would be nice.

He said that the physician advised against moving the inmate to the interview room, as the interrogation itself might be strain enough to crumble his fragile psyche.

She said that that's not what she meant by that. She tugged on her lanyard.

He smiled and made a motion with his hands. The guards stepped down the corridor, but not out of sight. Our escort waited by the cell door, but yielded space for us to enter.

She made for the cell, but I grab her wrist before she did and I motioned for the her to put on her mask as I put on my own.

She asked if we really needed them.

"No, but he will."

Our escort alerted the prisoner again and told us that we had ten minutes and that the cameras had been turned off momentarily so that we could conduct our interview. He made a weird face at our appearance and laughed as we walked down the corridor.

Behind a second wall of bars was the prisoner. He was sitting down on the cement stool that was permanently rooted near the foot of his cot bed. He was wearing the orange garb of the men of the Supermax, his risen frame revealing his bloated and fat waistline, like that of a pregnant cat. On his forehead was a mass of scar tissue shaped like a rudimentary crucifix, as if a toddler drew the alphabet with the opposite hand. His beard was below his rib cage, apparently uncut since when he was apprehended. His hair was wrapped in a ponytail and the thinning hairline two decades prior had blossomed into full-scale male pattern baldness.

The mask was soft, black leather, shipped in by the soldiers as an emasculating gag for the prisoners. The leashes, the dog collars, the chains. It all became public. It all leaked. This didn't. This was still mine.

"Hello, teacher. Have you come back to educate me again?"

His voice was soft, but not meek.

"It has been a while since our last lesson."

She moved in subtle, uncomfortable fidgets and jerks.

"Mister Yous …"

I cut her off. "Do you remember what I taught you last?"

"You were educating me on the true meaning of pain."

She moved in subtle, uncomfortable fidgets and jerks.

"Have you forgotten our last lesson?"

He ran his index finger across his forehead, his soft-fingers running along the divot at the intersection of the lines that he forced onto his flesh.

"No."

3. Franklin Pierce could only see Ambassador Ticonderoga when he was taking a bath. The Ambassador was very adamant that this was their arrangement.

"There are bugs everywhere. You never know who could be listening: the Ethiopians, naturally, it's their own country for God's sake, but it's not just them: the Saudis, the Gulf States, the Russians, the Chinese, your boys in DepCat, Liberals… Mark my words, the bathroom is man's last sanctuary. There are some morals that even the most lecherous men must observe. Every man has a code and it runs through their colon."

He had the State Department rip out the modern Eljer jet-pulse model bathtub, ostensibly as a debugging routine, but more as a remodeling. Speaking of the prior set up, Ambassador Ticonderoga called it "decadent" and soon had it replaced with a Wyatt Earp-era copper pot he had flown in from his private ranch near Jackson Hole, Wyoming. The rest of the bathroom was lined with course slate and the walls were boarded up with recovered pallet wood so as to "give the room life." The bathroom mirror was replaced with windows to nothing that were eventually white washed to "give *priv*acy to the privy," despite facing a large blank wall. The Ambassador justified it as an act of necessary symbolism catering to his "simple-kind of man" sensibilities. The whole affair cost the United States Government $150,000.

"Hey, when Uncle Sam is paying for dinner, I'm ordering Prime Rib," the Ambassador was fond of saying, "and if I'm footing my own bill, I'll be foraging in the forest eating roots, pine needles, edible berries and what not, fresh game, trout from the stream. They ought to have a constitutional ban against me, because these hands are lethal weapons."

The copper pot bathtub was so small that not all of Ambassador Ticonderoga could fit into it all at once. Legs and arms spilled over the other side and rested on the outer rim of the copper pot. The upper torso down to the armpit was left exposed and the Ambassador would have to ladle hot water and suds onto the un-submerged parts of his body. His fondness for Stetson Hats extended into bathtime and he'd leave the Stetson on his head, taking off his white hat only when disrobing or before ladling bathwater onto his head and scalp, usually the last act of the bath. He had mastered the trick of disrobing while keeping his shoes on, or at least the Larry Mahan's that oft occupied his feet, at least at first before he would kick them off using the one boot to take the other off before removing the last one with the assistance from the outer rim of the pot so as to brush in between the webs of his feet.

"You can come in, Francis. Ain't nothing you haven't seen before."

"Good afternoon, Ambassador."

Ambassador Ticonderoga let out a curt grunt. He was trying to take off his pants while keeping his Larry Mahan's on, a feat Franklin Pierce had seen him accomplish with grace and mastery countless times before, but, at present, a challenge that was giving him fits. The Ambassador was, as most diplomats are, middle aged. He would not be asked to model nude before freshman sculpture students anytime soon, but he was as comfortable in his own skin as just about anyone on earth could rightfully claim to be. The Ambassador finally got his Larry Mahan's through both pant legs and he lowered his body into the tiny bath, his rotund belly popping through the surface of suds like an island in the sea. He groaned with joy.

"Ahh, nothing in this world is better than a hot bath. Wouldn't you say?"

Franklin Pierce sat on a chair with his legs so close together he may as well be back in Bettendorf, Iowa, posing for his second-grade class picture. He wasn't sure if he was this way because the Ambassador was naked or what. It was definitely part of it. There was a certain bit of power the Ambassador held over him when he was in the bath. The ability to act casual when displaying vulnerability has the paradoxical bonus of making all those without all the more vulnerable themselves. Being naked amongst others ranking quite highly on Franklin Pierce's nightmare spectrum of vulnerability. The Ambassador's candid aloofness to the state of his own body projected a bulletproof sense of invincibility. He seemed to leech the self-confidence of others as he shed articles of clothing and when he was naked, you'd be gut hollow.

The Ambassador muttered quietly under his breath as he let the water warm his bones and soak his skin, what skin and bones were in the water at all. "Sinopec holdings. Chinese colonization. Political Islam. Insurgency. Counter-insurgency. It's all been foretold in the bits of the *Quran* I have glanced over. New world order. That kind of shit." And he trailed off as he was placid in the bath. "I need a pelt, Francis. I need a pelt."

"A pelt, sir?" For a moment Franklin Pierce thought he used pelt as some sort of Jackson Hole slang term for a towel and looked to his right and his left for a dry towel.

"We got to get us a terrorist, Francis. We got to get somebody. We need to show the people...we need to show the President that we are both doing our jobs. If you go out hunting, you can't go home without bringing home a pelt. You understand now? A pelt. A trophy. Something to mount upon the walls of the lodge … Your father didn't take you hunting, did he?"

"I grew up in the Quad Cities, sir. Bettendorf, Iowa. Along the Mississippi River. We went fishing a lot, my father and I."

"You catch anything big? A real prize catch?"

"Mostly Bluegills. Small fish. We ate what we caught, sir."

"Not that catch and release bull, eh? Waste not, want not. Spoken like a true American. Sort of like the man you were named after."

"I beg your pardon, sir?"

"Franklin Pierce. 14th President. Your namesake, no?"

"No, sir. My folks just liked the name, I guess. He wasn't that good of a president either."

"Underrated, Agent Pierce. Underrated. Did he like his drink too much? Sure, who hasn't? Did he try to placate the South to no avail? Sure, but would starting the Civil War 8 years earlier been a good outcome? Never, and I do mean never, underestimate just how many shitty Presidents there have been," and with a cupped hand and soft voice he said, "including this one, but you didn't hear that from me. No, Francis, your namesake is smack dab in a center of *blah*, not bad, not good, but, yes, underrated."

Ambassador Ticonderoga seemed to bubble up in the bathwater. "You see, this whole thing here in Ethiopia, the Ambassadorship, it ain't the end, it's the means to an end. I'm a patriot. I'm damn proud of it. To hell with the Ethiopians. America's the country I care about, Francis, the country I know. The real America, the true America, not what the government or the media or you DepCat spooks wants us to think, no offense."

"None taken, sir. Um? I'm sorry, do you still want a towel?"

The water spilled over the lip of the rim and onto the coarse slate below.

"You're not the sharpest tool in the shed, Francis, but you're my tool and I don't have many others like you. You, like this posting, are a means to an end, Francis. Yes, Francis, a means to end. Someday, we're gonna remake this world. No Gods. No Governments. Just Freedom."

The Ambassador removed his Stetson hat and placed it on the wet slate. The rim of the hat imprinted a red ring around his forehead and his thinning, gray hair was matted and disheveled. He cupped his hands and dumped the suds onto his scalp.

"A pelt, Francis. You're going to help get me my pelt," he said as he rose from the tub, the suds rolling down his big body, into his Larry Mahan's, and down onto the now slick slate.

"Now do you want a towel, sir?"

4. Edwards emerged up the steps from the subway and onto Canal. It was only 6AM, but the throngs of people were already out. The subways were full, sure. In yellow Checker cabs, and in the stream of bridge-and-tunnel commuters were out, but in the streets? The bums, the drifters, the foreign tourists, the cops, and the buskers? The soot-blasted air of the subway that weighed him down was lifted like an overcoat as he got street side. He took a moment to soak it in, to breathe it. Chinatown street vendors were getting back from midday smoke runs that started before the dawn. Rotisserie Peking Duck fresh in the window or old from the night before, nobody could tell. Sirens were more common than silence. For a brief moment, not even a second, past the wafts of fish scales, stale restaurant grease, gasoline, and aborted cigarettes, he could smell the sea. He tried to hold it for as long as he could, but the moment collapsed, so fleeting he thought he imagined it. He darted like he had some place to be, and he did. The old FBI Building on Worth and Broadway. His first day there. He'd have taken the bus down from Canal, but he was still relatively new to the city and didn't trust himself to time it right with the bus schedule.

He had odd, suburban fears of sitting at a ghetto bus stop and waiting for a ride that would never come. Lost, stranded in a concrete canyon so tall and cavernous the sun's light didn't reach the bottom of the pit. Waves of hucksters and con artists would nibble at his digits, trying to get in a bite. Soon enough, with blood in the water, the big fish would circle in. Pimps and mobsters of unknown origin, from countries not even on the map, not even of the same world. He clutched at his wrists with sweaty palms and assured himself that there was nothing to fear. This didn't affect him all that much living in D.C., since he was over at the Department of Catastrophe Management Headquarters in McLean. Still, he'd gotten used to it, city living, and slowly, step-by-step disarmed himself. It wasn't Mayberry, but he let his guard down from time to time, let his shoulders slack. Nevertheless, he knew that each city was its own beast and when he entered a new city he'd reset psychologically, and the old fears would re-emerge.

He had just moved into a DUMBO studio above a Greek bodega that had previously housed a storage for a local Pornographic Video Rental chain throughout the outer boroughs. They switched over to DVD's a few years back and could store them in half the square footage. So, they sent the old VHS's to landfill, and had a contractor re-do the top floor for new tenants. Edwards felt the exact same civic duty at gentrifying the former porno den that he did when he voted or when he prayed, like he was banishing some old ghost, burying it deeper and deeper into the strata of history.

Even riding the subway was a surprising joy. The feeling would be fleeting, even he knew that. The grind would eventually get to him. The daily traumas too potent and numerous to shield from burning itself like a permanent brand on his internal psyche, but for all the leering creeps and hopeless cases there were the nameless, voiceless throngs of people who went about their daily toil without doubt and without complaint every single day and outnumbered the deplorables 100:1. He enjoyed the hustle and bustle, of being a part of something instead of being apart. It was the basic trade off of city living, communal living for that matter, to gain access to the greater good meant gain access to that greater evil, smaller, but more potent, like Asp venom. He imagined old world caravans and wild west settlers banding together against raiding parties and knew that they were stronger together but wondered if it was that their strength made them vulnerable in the first place.

The old FBI building was just down Broadway and as he approached the plaza from the north, Edwards could see a crowd gathering outside of it. It didn't have the vibe of a plaza crowd. There was no flow to their movements, no direction. They were turgid, stagnant. He could see that they were behind police tape and New York City cops were manning the line keeping out passersby.

TV crews were parked across the street from the plaza. Cameramen and on-screen reporters negotiated angles of lighting and spots of pavement with rival crews from other networks. Newspaper vendors left their posts to check on the goings-on across the block. A NYPD van was escorted through the lines of yellow tape and it ran the curb into the crime scene, continuing until it reached the stair on the plaza. The big back doors opened up revealing a team of men in dark green HAZMAT suits with clear plastic visors, welded seams, and zipper entry. They slowly filed into the building's main entryway as the crowd began to marginally thin, onlookers uneasy with the prospect of being within eyesight of some breathable terror. For if you can see the men in the ventilated suits what the fuck are you doing standing there staring at them? Run.

Edwards approached the police line and asked a beat cop what was going on.

"Active crime scene," he said, "No one's going in."

"I'm with the Department. I've got to go in there."

"You got credentials?"

It was his first day in the New York office and even though he still had his DepCat badge, he knew that alone probably wouldn't get him clearance into a building in lockdown. Edwards showed the cop his badge anyway.

"Clearance? The place is in lockdown, sir. The entire building has already been evacuated."

"People are saying its Anthrax in the mailroom," said a woman at the police line next to him.

"Active crime scene," said the cop, "Nothing official yet."

Edwards eyed a bank of payphones on the street adjacent to where the reporters had set up base. His beeper hadn't gone off, but still he thought about calling the secretary's line to try and report in, but there was no one on the other line. The building was truly evacuated. He thought about calling Special Agent in Charge on his personal cell phone, but the pay phone lines might not be secure.

He walked mindlessly in purposeless haze. He had nowhere to go, nothing to do. He checked his beeper frequently and tried to match the pace of the tourists and the business folk in their hustle, lest he look like a loiterer. By the time he knew it, he had already taken Broadway past the City Hall Park and the cavalcade of squad cars that lined the perimeter of it. He paused for a second to admire the show of force by the police. For all he knew, the threat was nebulous. A package in the mailroom of a building just blocks away. An unknown substance, possibly Anthrax. Who really knew? Maybe the old lady was bullshitting. Maybe she was just misinformed, continuing a chain of falsehoods from some unknown and untraceable origin. Or maybe she had it on good authority. The team of investigators in HAZMAT suits seemed to support this line of thinking. What is more is that if the material were found in the mailroom then the suspect more than likely wasn't around. He sent it in the mail. The reflex to mobilize present, material forces in mass at a moment's notice. The men, the cars, the logistics, the choreography, all of it. Against what? An airborne, particle threat sent to another building blocks away by an unknown belligerent who could be a continent away. What was parked outside City Hall Park in a phalanx was instinct and impulse. It was as much for the men and women walking the street then for the men and women under specific threat.

One-way traffic rolled past his shoulder in turgid fits, as crushes of cars and buses came off of side street detours, the main drag of Broadway blocked off in front of the DepCat Headquarters. Throngs of pedestrian traffic meant that only a handful of motorists could make each successive green light. Sirens could be heard throughout as he made his way south down Broadway, into the Canyon of Heroes. He recalled the ticker tape parades from his youth that would sear into his memory as imprints of universal joy. Soldiers returning home from war, athletes returning home from long, successful seasons, politicians triumphing after ascending to the presidency: their rubber of their soles marched along that victorious road, or at least rode in open air cars that marched for them.

The last parade was a year ago. The Yankees had won their first World Series since 1978 after 18 years of semi-comic relevancy. Edwards was in the DepCat office in Virginia when he saw it playing on one of the office TV's several New Yorkers in the office had turned on. Edwards stood in the back as the New Yorkers rejoiced and the rest of the office workers went about their business. A co-worker from Atlanta lamented the Braves ill-fortune at losing three World Series within the decade, taking no solace in their title just one year prior. On screen, Wade Boggs, the old Red Sox third baseman, was riding a horse with an NYPD cop, just like he did after they clinched in Game 6. Streams of white ticker tape hung and sunk across the expanse between the concrete canyons like slacked power lines in barrio alleyways. It was all in color, but the gray October skies coupled with the great shadows cast by the scaling architecture down onto the street level created a muted lens through which everything was filtered through. The blue of the Yankees' caps and jackets seemed to turn pitch black like the Navy uniforms of the returning sailors on VE Day. Dark leather jackets and wool coats seemed to ratchet down to a sort of taupe. The views down street faded into the haze of oblivion, caught up in a fall fog rolling out just as the buses rolled in. The passersby onscreen congealed into a dark mass of jacketed arms, gloves, and hair, the occasional flash of pink skin and horned rim glasses breaking up the monotony of the whole. The color mostly came from the streetlights, the familiar green, yellow, and red still stuck in their routines as the parade cascaded southbound regardless of their prompts.

The sun was well up above the skyline today, but even then, Edwards could feel that darkened tone as he made his way southbound. He felt as if this particular urban landscape were stuck in time. Sure, the storefronts and advertisements changed. Gem Razors was swapped out for Gillettes, Ballentine Cigarettes for Marlboros, and the mom and pop drug stores or luncheonettes for CVS or Dunkin' Donuts or whatever, but the spirit of the street, the image, the tone was unchanged since back when, back during the end of the war, back before the war, even in technicolor, even in daylight.

Daylight, wide beams of morning sun would break through the black blocks in the wide intersections that ran East to West, breaking the line like a fissure in the bedrock and for a moment Edwards thought he was in a garden or a park. He could be anywhere but here. And then the light turned on the crosswalks and the little white icon of a man lit up and he was back in it again. He wasn't out of it until his eye gravitated towards something else, equally iconic. The twin towers of the World Trade

Center to the west, lit by the sun over the Atlantic, gleaming down Liberty Street from where Edwards stood at the corner of Zuccotti Park.

Edwards gave his beeper a cursory glance just to satisfy any possible anxiety or guilt at being unable to check into the office on his first day posted there. Nope. None. No one beeped. No one knew he was there. He'd call in later. Contact people he knew back in Virginia, former supervisors and case officers, who'd put him in contact with who he needed to be in contact with. He couldn't do anything until then, except take Liberty over to the feet of the Towers.

The Towers themselves were quite ugly. It was all slats of metal siding and vertical girders lined like pinstripes along a capo's suit up as the main body of concrete thrust upward and outward, almost infinitely from his perspective. Its imprint lingered in the outer background like a second and third moon as flocks of birds and wafts of street level steam orbited around it. Looking up at them felt as if existing in some sort of mirror plane, seeing the reflection and the reflector simultaneously. But which one was the original? Tower 1 or Tower 2? One of them had some sort of spire atop it. An antenna or weather tower maybe. Did it even matter? Edwards began to feel the impulse to divide, to halve the world in two, to formulate a meridian somewhere in between the lines of sidewalk crack that existed in the plaza between the two colossuses. East and West. North and South. The Future and the Past. The living and the dead. Everyone else was oblivious to this or handled it in their own way. As if they had long since experienced what Edwards felt in some knowing, yet unarticulated way and simply went on about their day in full, but silent recognition of the colossuses and their effects.

Walking onto the plaza, Edwards felt a sort of vertigo. He paused momentarily and took his eyes off the skyscrapers, trying to get his bearings, but it wouldn't cease. In fact, staring at the ground seemed to make things worse. He felt not as if he were on solid ground at the foot of two large buildings, but somehow exactly in the middle. Staring back up at the towers, he felt the gravity of the space they occupied. He felt as if the original column of air from the buildings was suddenly and unexpectedly transferred upon him, the full weight of the voided space. He began to imagine the depth of the towers projected downward into the ground, past the sewer lines and the subway tunnels, down into what lied beneath.

An image of the underground was in his mind. An image from the '93 bombing. The Ramzi Yousef bombing. It only killed six people, but it could have been so much worse. He was trying to play dominoes, Yousef was, taking out the legs out of one tower and knock it into the other. The image on the front page of the papers was of the bombed-out car park: the twisted steel and the ticker tape ribbons of rebar that were strung about. The faces of six who died were there too, seared into his memory: a businessman who happened to park on the same level as the Ryder truck with a 1,300-pound bomb in it and the five Port Authority officers pancaked by a collapsing wall on the same floor. They could have caught him then. Yousef lit the bomb with a 20-foot fuse and walked away. He was in the building and just walked away. Into the streets. Onto Broadway walking against traffic. The Bojinka attacks, the downing of the airplanes, the interventions, the unilateral invasions, all of it could have been avoided if someone had been able to nab him right then and there. Still, it could have been much worse. The towers could have fallen.

"It's beautiful, no?" said an older foreign tourist, maybe an Austrian or a German.

"Yeah, it's something else." said Edwards, the act of talking to someone, anyone, grounded him in the moment, giving him gravity. He checked his beeper again and, sure enough, it was beeping. He put it back into his pocket and made for Tower One and a telephone inside.

Jim Johnson
Wild

What is wild? In Minnesota, the state of hockey, the professional team is named The Wild. But is Minnesota wild? Is anything wild anymore?

Minnesota is wild. Wolves are wild, as are beavers, brook trout, and blueberries. If blueberries, fertilized by blackflies, then blackflies. Osprey, eagles, and moose. Shrews. Mosquitos, of course. Moccasin flowers. White pines and northern white cedar. Walleyes in rivers, in lakes. Northern pike. Lake trout in only the remotest lakes. But not rainbow trout planted in lakes. Or splake hybrids.

Or are they too wild?

Why not in cold water, tall-tree-lined lakes at the end of the road?

Technically, planted fish are not considered wild. But didn't their inherited makeup, their DNA, kick in right after their arrival (dropped from float planes, tossed out of buckets) into wild waters take over? No longer able to pluck pellets like delivered pizzas, but now left to chase zigging mayflies, zagging dragonfly nymphs, easy scuds, scuttling crayfish, even late-night shrews. With enough discrimination to turn up their speckled snouts at nightcrawlers threaded onto #4 eagle claw hooks tied to a fifteen-pound test monofilament while suspended from red and white bobbers with disinterest and a polite, No thank you. Another dragonfly nymph, please, should do. Unless a plump brown shrew should drop in out of the shadows.

Of course there will be binges. Just before the warm electric landlady thunder storms after a hot day in July. Or an evening of hexagenia mayflies suddenly appearing like angels (hence hex angels). But knowing how to hangout under cutbanks and fallen logs, among roots, hidden in the clear as a mirror sky. No wind. Ospreys cruising dangerously, even the loons call security.

One calm idyllic day in September my friend Dave fished a small trout-stocked lake named, of course, Lucky. The day so calm the local osprey even knew it was too nice to fish. Instead the powerful fishhawk flew from white pine to white pine karate kicking the dead lower branches until each fell to the ground. Some were logs the size loggers on a good night see in their dreams.

Osprey nests are huge, made of better lumber than all the jazz clubs in the French Quarter of New Orleans pieced together with drift from the delta. Osprey nests are a similar size, large enough for mom, dad, and 2 or 3 not-so-little ones squawking about not having been fed for an hour wondering when dad will bring back another hefty fish.

But this was rebuilding day. The black masked osprey patriarch picked up each broken off branch and carried it gripped in talons back to the nest where mom would then insist on more and back would go dad, flying trip after trip to satisfy she who insists on bigger, though their home was already complete with a lake view, until eventually the heavy logs took their toll. Osprey papa lost his grip and down came a log, landing with a terrible splash not less than 2 feet away, according to Dave, from Dave afloat in his float tube in the middle of Lucky Lake.

Oops, sorry. Sorry, Mom, and back went father osprey for yet another log. And again directly over Lucky Lake, the tired talons let go.

Dave decided not to depend upon Lucky Lake's name being fortuitous and slowly finned toward the shore. It wasn't, though even I'm sure that osprey would rather have gone fishing, a good fishing day, too bright and calm.

Yet it was wild.

Isn't this experience the unknown we always fish for, casting cast after cast into new waters? And for each new day even old waters are new (see Roderick Haig Brown and zen). So we fishermen are always casting into the wild. The wild out there. The wild unknown.

I know it is why I walk a stream to fish a hole I have never been to before, one that from where I stand looks like it could be good, so I go on, even though the walk is long. Over and around large boulders. The bank thick with underbrush, so thick I stay in the stream, always in the stream, around large rocks, carefully over the smooth and slippery, carrying my fly rod in one hand, an old ski pole to maintain balance in the other, or no ski pole, using that hand to grab onto alder branches. Then I finally get to that pool that looked so good from a distance: too slow, too shallow, too wide. But ahead in the distance just beyond the next bend what looks like a rapids falling into a narrow pool. So I go.

And on.

Into the wild, or wilder, because I want to know.

Folk Opera Book Review

Text for Our Nomadic Future
(Red Dragonfly Press, 2018)

A new collection of poems by Jim Johnson

The wild, former Duluth Poet Laureate Jim Johnson notes in the introduction to a slender new collection packed with careful observation, is something he wanted to write about back when he first attempted poetry. In this, his ninth book, Johnson goes well beyond writing about the wild to giving it voice, a text. The wild speaks in broken lines like these from THAT NIGHT:

> That night the loons called
> back and forth
>   forth and back
> across the lake the proclamation
> so ancient, so wild, so unconscious
> only they could say,

the ice is out. The ice is out. *Ja,*
the ice is out.

Text for Out Nomadic Future is itinerant, a wandering northward, wondering about the south. "Chicago," he says, "is north to the blues." Rain speaks, as in this untitled jewel from the section Northern Minnesota Web of Gems:

Rain as the sound of rain falling
on an oil drum
rather than an old man sobbing
read like a black book
reindeer or raven ridden from the other world
returned as from the dead
rippled as an otter's slide
rivers speaking in tongues

The voices of the wild are the *Text,* animated transcriptions that move back and forth/forth and back from organism to human, from human to terrestrial—the arboreal, rill, quag and lake smooth agates. "It's easy to love a wet rock," Johnson says in ALONG LAKE SUPERIOR, nudging his blank verse beyond anthropomorphism to grand singularity, something perhaps only found in "the other world" where the organic and the non-organic form a unified planetary ecosystem. "Lay me down on laurel, Labrador tea, / and leatherleaf," he instructs IN LOVE ME LIKE A bog. "Lay me across sphagnum moss, solomon's seal / and rosemary."

Unflinching observation, attention to minute detail notwithstanding, Johnson's greatest skill is the lyric of identification—testifying to the existence of all things as in THE GREAT BLUE HERON RETURNS TO THE NORTH:

… a long-necked question mark
at a backwoods bar asking, *Do you have any*
Chardonnay? maybe standing midstream
until the woman in the too-tight Chainsaw
Sister T-shirt clutching three bottles of
Leinenkugels in each hand and slamming
them down onto the bar like an exclamation
to the point, *This is a hard drinking beer*
drinking north woods saloon. We don't serve
any wine whatsoever. So the great blue
heron, chewing the frog hopper caught
sideways in its yellow mandibles, pauses
and spits it out right there on the sawdust
floor.

Johnson would have us save the planet, believers and deniers, by moving south to north, a herder-gatherer, listening to its voice, reading its *TEXT.*

The song of the white-throated sparrow
sure enough is
the text for our nomadic future.

Text for Our Nomadic Future is agate, lake and bog, an other-world, a splendid Baedeker for the spirit that roams. —Tom Driscoll

Micheal Akutagawa
from The Homer Nods

Invocation

BODIES, I have in mind. Definitely,
most especially, YOURS! EMBODIMENT,
as well. You GODS know the trick, and you know
what poor wankering FOOLS we are in the wake
of it all. I ask your help--since you cause
or at least condone it, for your amusement,
perhaps. Inspire ME! Let ME sing--better
than I typically do! Let ME cop the secret,
and, MAYBE, cop that HEAVENLY feel again!

Tell of that man, a writer WANNA-BE,
a "Poet", who usually fretted or
footled around—resourceful hankerer.
A dandy word or image swatted at,
a verbal bauble snatched for, "ideas",
papered plans and intentions, nor dispersed,
persistent as summer's black gnats in Maine.

Yet not by sputtered fits of WILL alone,
nor lurching starts of callous'd Muse-abuse
is such honey'd Verse made that might outlast
the "Best Bought By" date of honey'd donuts.

Namely, of THOSE proroguings, GODS, tell US—
supernumeraries. BEGIN, then,
at whatever point in the story you WILL—
Let stem STAINS stereo!

Book 5

Peerless in Olympian pulchritude,
Penelope stretched her arms above her head;
she was, after all, so tired. And though her lips
parted in a yawn, they met in a smile
as she remembered right then the bijoux
and the baubles that her new beaux had bought—
Ivyed scions, L. L. Bean prep replete;
naturally, frat-boys, WammaGammaMu;
handsome and now promise-wet behind

their Kaplan-coached undergrad cum laude ears;
young men lantern-jawed, bright-eyed and wire-rimmed,
offering "Love" (and associate accounts
at Tiffany, Nordstrom, and at Bloomingdale's)
under a just-so paper a cappello-
harmonied blue moon and paper-lanterned stars.

She sighed, then gathered her doubloon-blonde hair
from her alabaster shoulders, gently
twisting it into a loose and honey'd knot.
Very lightly, next, she slipped into bed,
then fluffed, then drew the pillows closely about.
Her dainty right foot she slid along the edge
of the queen-sized mattress and designer covers,
while the moonlight, a lullaby, gently
slanted through the casement window. And soon,
Penelope slept—

         as Homer, better versed
in indolence than in WRITING any Verse,
lay flopped and slack on the IKEA couch.

There was only the doodled fill, then fall,
fill, then fall of the printed window curtains,
and a dazed and aimless lightning bug that kept
bumping again, again, against the window screen.

Suddenly, there was a frightful clanking,
as out of the moonlight stepped WILLIAM SHAKESPEARE!

But not as Homer had dreamed him before—
cracker-chested, that upstart crow, a dweeb
in a pink and fuchsia Speedo swimsuit,
prancing around and pursing like Mick Jagger,
yet ALWAYS churning words for his Honey'd Verse.

This time, bundled head-to-toe in burnished
armor, having just finished dress rehearsal
of likely yet another hit play written,
they said, sans Will's having blotted out a line.

Its plot was a horrific manufacture
of carnal, bloody, and unnatural acts,
of accidental judgments, casual slaughters,
of deaths put on by cunning and forced course,
and, in this upshot, purposes mistook,
and then fallen on the inventors' heads.
A play wherein its author plays the "Ghost".

Thus, he eyed Homer, and let out with a spooky peal—

"Mwaaaa ha ha ha haah!"

Ghost/Writer William Shakespeare then solemnly
held aloft a black Mont Blanc pen, and beckoned
dolorously for Homer's un-severed attention.

"Homer", the feigned 'Ghost' said in a spectral voice,
"the hour is almost come when I to that theatre
and its critics—unearthly, dark and supernatural—
must at last render myself up for performance
and review. Mark me. Marshal thy observance
to all that I shall unfold to you: WRITE!

Desist from your promises and your plans,
those windy suspirations of forced breath.
Quit your proclamations of resolve—and WRITE!
Assume a virtue, if you have it not!"

Homer stared, befuddled, in his nightcap
and "You Don't Know Diddley" Nike t-shirt,
but further on the Apparition spoke.

"I am come now both for your prompting AND
as your confederate! An epic poem
can't be too heavy, nor haiku too light.

But, list, Homer! List! O list! Tried and true,
evergreen, in fact, is 'Compare and Contrast',
the elemental grist for high school English
class themes. Next, are 'Symbols Found, then Deciphered',
and 'How I Spent My Summer Vacation'.

Here is a variation—re: the lyrics
for The Beatles song, called 'Norwegian Wood'.

I pronounce it that Lennon wrote the song
with my play, *Hamlet*, in mind.

             It's OBVIOUS.
And, there, in fact, is your topic sentence!

The NORWEGIAN (i.e., Fortinbras) WOULD—
and did! WOULD, as in want to, try to,
might be expected to. And WOOD, as in furniture,
furnishings.

       Get it?

       Turns out that Hamlet

was there out-Heroding Herod because
young Fortinbras, a guy very high on
the dork-o-meter, COULD, so why oh why
couldn't HE?

Furthermore, the woman
in the first stanza is OBVIOUSLY
Ophelia. (And I'll tell you something else:
Lennon was perceptive enough to be
among the first to know that the word play
with her name was, 'I'll feel ya!')

Long story short,
that verse, and those that follow, parallel
the distemperature of the Hamlet family.

Homer, buddy, am I going too fast for you?

But, soft, methinks I scent the morning's air.
Therefore, to return to this pointed brief,
brief let me be. For thus, to continue,
in fact, was junior so upset. Comparison
between *Hamlet* and 'Norwegian Wood' goes on
from there.

OBVIOUSLY.

Now I will admit
that Lennon could write some oblique lyrics,
in contrast to the simpleton ditties
of Paul and Ringo.

I mean, really,
'Michelle ma belle, sont les mots qui vont
très bien ensemble'? It's SOOOOO heavy!
I was writing that kind of French for laughs
in *Henry the Fifth*.

And here's another
thing in 'Norwegian Wood' that probably
escaped you. I quote: 'She showed me her room.
Wasn't it good, Norwegian Wood?'

You've heard
of IKEA furniture? Lennon foresaw
those Scandinavian and ill-fated '80s
yuppie labors. You know—all those flat-packed
furnishings, and mighty travailled allen-key
wrenchings.
Which was, of course, how the apartment

in the song was furnished.
       And—had there been
an IKEA branch shop in Stratford-upon-Avon
for MY wife, Anne, HATH-A-WAY with credit cards—
doubtless where we'd have gotten our second
best bed.

    But look not so apoplexed, Homer.
Who's more to believe? Murray the K?
Brian Epstein? The Maharishi?
Your high school English teacher?
       Holy
Instant Karma, for Christsakes (whom The Beatles
DID become bigger than—once again, just like
Lennon said):

    Get on the Yellow Submarine!

Quickly, Homer, do NOT delay. Get this
impartment written up ASAP,
and post it posthaste where I will direct.

As a DARK LADY, who shall remain nameless,
once said of some sonnets I footled over—

  'To pick up the rhyme, you gotta do the time!'

So fare thee well at once. The glow-worm shows
the morning to be near. Adieu, adieu,
Homer: REMEMBER ME. The rest is silence."

Then mournfully reprising in reverse
the lack of liquefaction with which he
appeared, he clanked and clattered his way
back through the moonlight, leaving a copy
of *THE SHAKESPEARE QUARTERLY*—where dog-eared
was a call for academic papers
on the topic, "Shakespeare in Performance:
Some Cultural Repercussions and Riffs".

Now there was on Homer's IKEA table
a typewriter, a secondhand Underwood,
present from Eurycleia Yoko-san,
that kindly old charwoman, a widow.

Her husband, too, wanted to be a "Poet",
but had worn out not even a single
typewriter ribbon in 40-odd years,
nor so much as the cartridge to a pen.

"Homer", she'd said, "Take this—and do better!
It would make ME feel better, if you did."

Whereupon, as schoolboys swerve from their school books,
Homer went un-swerved to that very typewriter.

He rolled a blank sheet of moon-white paper
into the ancient black Underwood, and—
miraculously, as if the exposition
were writing itself, page after charged page
it came camera-ready from the typewriter;
furthermore, perfectly conforming to
the Modern Language Association's
Handbook for Writers of Research Papers.

Homer had no need for a wastebasket,
nor did he need to blot out a single line.
He had only to keep pace with the keys
as they released to the paper the words
which became the scholarly manuscript
entitled, "This Bard Has Flown: William Shakespeare,
The Beatles, *Hamlet*, and 'Norwegian Wood.'"

The sky, then, cracked with a wondrous lightning bolt—
a blazing sign!
        And Homer fell sweetly
to sleep, amidst his sharpened Faber pencils,
his unemployed erasers, his Mont Blanc pen, and
the pages of moon-white paper, now NOT blank.

Meanwhile, top-heavy treading celestial boards,
back to rehearsal went Writer/Ghost Will Shakespeare.

Hrithik Rana
The Dream Pill

Jeremy looked at the ceiling with his eyes squinted. The patterns were back. The reoccurring blue and black dots, moving in an arbitrary dance, emitting little flashing strokes of light and when vanishing leaving a little faded remnant of the light. Looking like floating dust. He has been an insomniac for last two months. Nothing was working, honeycomb was ineffective, alcohol made him angrier and recently he tried pot. John was the guy who would go to jail if cops check his place. The acupuncture didn't get him anything, only cost a couple hundred bucks, and didn't get him high either. Life seemed to be turned upside down.

Sleeplessness somewhat stopped him from writing his papers. He wanted to become a writer, but before his insomnia he went through writer's block, and this disease didn't help it. Hallucinations started in the second month. Lights, little strokes of electricity in the surroundings, bear walking across his room, bear he can hear but can't see.

Born in a town of Mt. Jakpit, Jeremy had been a good son. He was the only kid

Adapted from photo by Bady Qb - upsplash

in the house. Tom and Martha gave their all to raise this man. Tom was a farmer and Martha taught in a local community college. Growing up he was a healthy kid, played basketball, wrote for the school's column, dated a lot of girls, and then graduated high-school with a 3.2 GPA. He got a full scholarship to study in the University of Batencross, but his parents asked him to stay with them as he was the only son. Soon after he refused the college programme Martha and Tom died during a road trip to Palenjade when the bus slipped and fell in a river.

The trauma his mind went through was everlasting. He developed some habits and routines and stuck to them. He started going on long walks, started smoking cigarettes, trying drinking, stopped going to college and started writing instead. One evening he was sitting on a bench in the Parker Avenue and thought about working on some ideas he had as a teenager. His notepad was full of random stuff and then he started working on them. In 4 months, he left the place and went to The Oaks, a city which is famous for writers.

At first, he had a tough time finding a job to pay for his dream, he had no college degree. Going to a college would be expensive, and he didn't want to sell his parent's property. At last he found a waiter's job in Bakers on Barol Street. He made acquaintance with John.

He was lying on his bed, looking at the fragments of his mind dancing in front his eyes. He could do nothing else. Didn't wanted to write, couldn't sleep.

Outside the 113A, The Barol Street, snow covered the sidewalks. Sweepers did a good job sweeping the stuff off the road. Every corner was given a sweeper to prevent any accidents. The crime city of the country had been quiet from a long time. People were happier, but not Jeremy.

It was 11PM when John closed the Bakers.

"Good night, man. I hope you get some sleep"

Jeremy bent his left knee to put the key in the lock."

"Yeah. Hope so," Jeremy said as he got up, moved a little right and bent to lock the right side of the shutter.

"You trying them pills? Hagwot's a hell of a man I tell you. His stuff get you high. Get you really high," John's tongue was touching the left corner of his mouth and he was looking at the upper right corner as he was digging his pockets. When his hands were out, he had a small piece of paper, which fell on the ground, and a zip-lock which had some pills in it.

"None of your shit, tough guy", Jeremy shook both of the locks to make sure they were locked.

He saw the packet and gasped.

"What are these? Ecstasy?"

"Some pills Hogwot gave me," John said with a smirk on his face. "They helped me through some tough days … nights, tough nights."

"They help you get sleepy? Man, I have tried pot, even pot fails to get me a nap, I don't think this'll help."

"Give it a shot."

"Okay." Jeremy dug in his back pocket and took out his wallet. "How much for one pill?"

"Friends don't business. Take it my friend."

John gave the packet to Jerr.

"So what do it do to you?"

"It's kind of an introspective pill. You will dream and everything you see will be symbolic. It's interesting to break it down yourself. You come to know how much you know the world and yourself."

"This is so weird, man. This constant weariness is killing me."

"Your face tells your story, brother." He took out a pack from his back pocket and brought it close to his face, took one cigarette using his incisors, nodded towards Jeremy who shook his head. He then put the pack back where it was. He took out the lighter and clicked it. It protested thrice, finally giving the light the fourth time. John took a big puff, inhaled deeply.

"There's one thing about this world. Everything talks", He said. Smoke came out of his mouth like breath.

"So you are Sigmund Freud now?"

"Haha," John gave a little laugh, "Nah, man. This pill is magical. You see stuff and it will break itself down. It got its own ways. It's like that ring in the Lord of the Rings."

"I can't wait to see what this does to me." He took the pills out and looked at them.

"Tell me about it tomorrow," John said as he started walking across the road.

"Okay see you tomorrow then," Jeremy said. He put the packet in his chest pocket.

Jeremy just stood there in silence for a couple of seconds. Two dogs started growling and one had his head in a trash bin trying to fetch something for himself. Jeremy faked picking up a stone. Dogs backed a little and then came to their initial position, barking this time. Crickets chirping felt calming. Jeremy looked at his room's window and thought about how he will spend the night tonight.

It was 1 mile from The Bakers to the Pavilion bus stop. Most of the distance they walked together in silence. Sometimes John would ask Jeremy about the girls who come every evening to do some paperwork and Jeremy would tell him about what they ordered and that he got no chance with them so bother not trying to go with his stupid face and impress them. Two months earlier, Jeremy had rented the upstairs room of the restaurant to crash in. Since then, John walked alone to the bus stop.

He glanced at his watch—11:29.

Jeremy was sitting on his chair. His back a little curved forward to eat the burger he packed for himself. The ketchup dripping from the bottom of the patty as he took a bite from it. The whole thing was drenched in tomato ketchup.

After getting done with his dinner, Jeremy tossed the napkin in the bucket, got up and lifted his jacket to toss it on the ground to make space for himself to sleep. He heard a sound of the packet in his jacket and recalled those pills John had given him to try. He lifted it, checked the right pocket first, no pills were found, then the left pocket and there they were, in a transparent plastic bag. Sealed. He took the water bottle from the table to wash down the pills. Two pills he took that day. Two blue pills.

The night Jeremy had those pills, he fell asleep. The last time he fell asleep was a long time ago. Days since his last good night were nothing but one dreadful long night without any relaxation to his mind.

The last time he had a dream was farther away than the last time he fell into a deep healthy sleep. And the night he had those pills, he dreamed.

Jerr found himself standing in the middle of nowhere. He had a wifebeater on. The denim shirt he was wearing had all the buttons open. The imaginary six pack abs were nowhere to be found like any other imaginary things. His brown boots were drenched in mud, and his jeans had splashes of horse feces. He hadn't felt this energetic from a long time. Hell, he wasn't even able to get a nap. He was in a field which grew nothing, a plain ground surrounded by other ploughed fields.

The overhead sun was gazing his warmth down the earth. Birds flying in a V formation the leaders in the front and weaker behind. There were big gigantic rocks which formed the boundary of the fields. Trespassing was welcomed with a trash mouth and (If things get heated) with a gunshot to the head.

Jeremy held his palm over his head and tried to see where he was. Some two fields away was a man sitting on a chair. He was reading a newspaper. The fat gobbly figure seemed to be smoking a cigar. The big fat figure of the man was shaking like a fire in a chimney. The space around him in rotatory motion lacked any auditory illusion.

Then someone struck a distant tower bell, which radiated a wave covering everything around it like water. The tower was a high needle sort of thing. It was old, rusty, and had a broken structure. It was bent to the left, just a little, the top pointing at the mountains which were in the range of Jeremy's vision.

He was standing on a raised platform of a barn. He heard someone playing an acoustic guitar inside. The door to the barn was made of wood. It was a door of low maintenance. The wood was swollen in places. It creaked when he carefully turned the knob with his right hand and forced the door forward a little with his left shoulder, then stopped. He placed his ears firmly on the door. He listened to the guitar, unable to register the melody in his head. The tune wafted out of the little keyhole and passed through him the way water passes through a filter. He could feel his brain thumping behind his eyes.

Jeremy pushed open the door. There were two harpoons with blood on their top. The floor had a big red spot as if someone was stabbed and was kept here for some time. He turned to the door and went outside.

In front of him was the gate to the field. There was a car parked next to it, Red Sedan, newly polished, a dog was sleeping on its top. Jeremy looked to his left and saw a guy plowing the field. "Hey, man!" he went to him. His one arm held up in the air, trying to make himself as visible as possible. The guy was sitting on his knees and using a wooden stick to dig a hole on the ground like a dog who hides his bones.

"Can you please tell me what this place is?" The man looked up at him, his left palm over his head. His eyes were squinting and analyzing the man standing in front of him.

"You are nowhere. We all are in your head." And with that the man vanished in the air like smoke. "Wait, what?" the smoke rose in the air and was swept away by the wind. He couldn't believe what happened before his eyes. He was terrified. Chill went down his spine and his legs started shaking. His heart started thumping against his chest, protesting against it, to get out of the cavity and shoot itself out. He looked for the fat man who was reading a newspaper and couldn't see him anymore. The house he was sitting in now looked like a much distorted visual. It looked like the insides of a washing machine, the drum spinning at the speed of light. He looked down for the hole and couldn't find any.

"What is this place?" he cried and ran towards the Sedan.

Driving felt a little good. He was still thinking about the vanished man and how had he turned into smoke, the fat man and his house was another mystery which filled his mind. He glanced up into his rearview mirror and saw at least two miles of road behind him. Streets of Philadelphia played on the stereo.

He had covered at least 10 miles and yet he was to see another human. Driving faster he saw the milestone which said 'The grave of our brave cops.' It gave him a feeling of déjà vu. As turned his gaze forward he found himself parked in the driveway of a small house. It seemed to be a one room house. "Let's see where this goes."

There were wooden stairs who led to a raised platform. He peeked outside and the farms and fields were gone. There lay darkness in front of him. The view was of a night street whose lamps didn't work. There was a garbage bin and liquid was leaking from it. A mouse came running from underneath it and ran to the left corner. It was a big rat; jerr thought it was a small rabbit.

"Hey! Anybody home?" he went inside without waiting for an answer. It was pretty clear to him that this was a one room apartment and if anybody was here they'll know about an intruder before any greetings from him. There was a little counter on the left which was made into a kitchen. The drawers were left open. Everything else was well organized and in place. There was a chimney next to a chair which he supposed was meant to be a reading chair. Two bookshelves were across the room. Majority of the stationary were files, which gave Jeremy a feeling of déjà vu. He felt a deep connection to this place. It was tidy, full of books, and had wooden flooring. Behind the chair was a window which Jeremy didn't notice before. Day light was illuminating the room through it. He rushed to the door.

Jeremy was standing on the entry to the restaurant he was working in. John gave him that pill here in front of the gate. The day was bright. The surroundings were crowded. This was the rush hour.

Jeremy looked to his left and found a man who was walking away from him. From his clothes and the way he walked, he looked like John. Jeremy rushed towards him.

"John! Hey!"

He grabbed his shoulders and turned him. "What the."

A figure stood in front of him, about 5 feet-seven, wearing the same clothing as John. The same cap, the same denim shirt, and the same cargo pants. But the face was not of John, it was no body's face, there was no face. The figure's face looked like a horse's face but sometimes it looked like a red beard. Another illusion. The denim sleeves were folded. The hair that of a punk rock star.

"Where am I? What is this place?"

Suddenly his brain starting thumping and he fell down but ended up landing on a bed.

A thought occurred in his mind, *Your face is your identity.*
I am sure it was John, but what's wrong with his face? he asked himself.

Then like a hammer, he realized that the man who vanished in a smoke had no face either and the fat man's face didn't look intact.

"What about me? What about my face?" He got up from bed and ran to the mirror. Stood there looking at the floor, at his feet and then looked straight ahead and saw a figure with his body but no face at all. He couldn't see his face, it looked like an unknown galaxy gazing at itself. He didn't feel like a human anymore.

The surroundings started distorting. It looked like a big mess of illusions. A cluster of thick liquid put in a coffee blender. It started rotating anticlockwise and then clockwise. Everything seemed to be out of the capability of his eyes to analyze this and make him see this scenery of dream through his eyes. Finally, the puddle gave a glow and Jeremy woke up. Jeremy woke up. He woke up with a realization. Everything in the dream seemed to be reasonable now. *Our face is our identity*, in our mind of course. He had this line for his new essay in his head.

"I think I was not able to see their faces because I don't know who people really are. Our face is our identity. I guess I don't even know myself"

He took out his Mac and started writing down his analysis of the dream.

G. L. Rockey
The Fish House

Spending my summer vacation in New Orleans, my sperm-father, Leo Mancuso, had the balls to come to The Fish House.

Let me explain.

Shortly after I (Rick Allan) just turned eleven, school out for summer break, my non-sperm-father, Sid Allan, five six, medium build, receding black hair slicked back and parted on the left, the owner of a popular New Orleans restaurant, The Fish House, had me, on a bright summer morning, outside washing the canopy over his restaurant's front entrance. I'm up on a seven-foot stepladder with brush and bucket of water scrubbing away when I notice a green car pull

Photo by Zubair Khan-upsplash

into The Fish House parking lot and stop. After a few seconds, out of the car steps a man dressed in casual military uniform, long sleeve tan shirt, tan pants, black shoes, walking toward me.

The man getting closer, I recognize him from, when I was a few years younger, a couple meetings, photos in a scrapbook, all that, it's my sperm father, Leo Mancuso.

Smiling, he waves, steps closer, says, "Hello, hi, how are ya." Something like that.

I climb down from the ladder, we shake hands, blah blah blah for a few minutes when out of The Fish House front door appears Leo's ex (now married to my step father, Sid Allan) my mother, Carmella, slim, forty-four, brunet, former waitress. Smiling, she and Leo exchanged airport-screener type greetings.

Greetings over, we three went inside The Fish House and sat at a four top (that's a table that seats four) window table.

Yak yak and shortly thereafter, my non-sperm father, Sid, showed up.

Introduction, more airport screener greetings, Sid sat with us, five or so minutes of yak yak pass and a girl (The Fish House called the all-female food servers, "Girls.") came to the table, smiled demurely, leaned over and whispered something in my mother's ear.

Anxious look from my mother, she excused herself, and left.

My mother gone, we three boys yakked some more (mostly Leo and Sid) and in around a few minutes later my mother, pale as a virgin ghost, came back to the four-top table, sat where she had sat before, and, exchanging irritable-bile-syndrome glances, she said to Leo, "Aunt Fruma is upstairs having a cow. You gotta get the fuck out-a here, now." She didn't really say that, she said, nice as can be, "Aunt Fruma is very upset, you'll have to leave."

So you'll know, Aunt Fruma, eyes and ears everywhere, was Sid's aunt, owned The Fish House.

So you'll also know, after Sid's mother (Fruma's sister) died when Sid was just a tike, Aunt Fruma gained custody from Sid's father, became his guardian, made Sid manager of The Fish House when he was twenty something.

As to Aunt Fruma upstairs having a cow; she lived in an apartment above The Fish House. Her first husband, Jacob Nussbaum, who founded the restaurant umpteen years ago, died (they say from a fish bone stuck in his wind pipe) when he was fifty something. Shortly thereafter, Aunt Fruma sole owner of The Fish House, married the head of a local construction company, Anthony (Big Toe) Arcurio, who among other things dug holes around The Big Easy.

Anyway, back to Aunt Fruma having a cow.

Didn't take a jackeroffer to figure it out, my sperm father was in her restaurant, sitting at one of her restaurant tables, drinking coffee out of one of her cups, chatting with her daughter-in-law, his ex-wife, my mother, Carmella, and me. Not to mention, Sid, joining in.

Anyway, after an awkward whew moment, Leo gone, I went back outside to my ladder and bucket; Sid went back to doing whatever he was doing in the back-of-the-house (that's restaurant talk for the kitchen area), and Carmella went upstairs to calm Aunt Fruma.

Jon Welsh
Inside the State Funeral of George Herbert Walker Bush

Georgetown, January 7, 2019. Heads of State and other world leaders, including 5 former U.S. Presidents, political leaders across nations and parties, a panoply of religions, a host of peoples, all with common purpose: to pay respects to George H.W. Bush, the 41st President of the United States of America.

The perimeter begins at the Omni Shoreham hotel, where guests—many of the 3,000 attending the memorial service—queue for a luxurious bus ride under police escort to the heavily secured neighborhood and grounds of the Washington National Cathedral.

Streets for blocks around the cathedral's 57-acre site are blocked by snowplows and other heavy trucks. Pedestrians have one entrance, and the closest a taxi or Uber gets them is a good two blocks away. Our caravan is waved through. We drive onto the cathedral grounds, disembark and enter the cathedral's main doors beneath the Rose Window before 9:30 am, leaving 90 minutes to mill about, making conversation and greeting others before the memorial service.

The confluence of power and privilege. Condoleezza Rice—a few feet away, yet I couldn't get close enough to ask her if she's still playing the piano. Joe Biden—a grip'n'grin after I shook

Former President Jimmy Carter. (Photo by Jon Welsh.)

Jimmy Carter's hand and chatted with him for a minute. Karl Rove. I kept two rows between us. Colin Powell. Leon Panetta. A stoic James Baker, who breaks into tears when Dr. Russell Levenson, pastor of St. Martin's Episcopal Church in Houston, tells a parable of Baker massaging George Bush's feet and evoking a smile from a dying man.

At 10:30 we're asked to sit and a musical prologue takes us to the United States Capitol, now appearing on the big screens. We watch the president's casket leave the rotunda, the feet of the Honor Guard as they bear his body down the steps,

the family silent in the brisk air as the hearse receives its charge, the motorcade as it starts making its way across town and up the hill to where we are in attendance.

—20 minutes to reflect.

I recall Bush's unfailing graciousness and thoughtfulness, his humor and humility, his visceral competitiveness. I thought how fortunate we were with a president who now personifies greatness simply because he handled it with humility and grace. Bush knew how a president should behave, and his death reveals how much respect a leader with a moral compass can earn. Even in life he earned our respect: in the last twenty presidential elections, his 53% of the popular vote was exceeded only by Reagan, Nixon, Johnson, Eisenhower, and Franklin Roosevelt, and his approval rating after Operation Desert Storm evicted Saddam Hussein from Kuwait reached a stratospheric 89 percent.

But the gilded resume and laurel wreaths for helping Nixon open China, passing the Clean Air Act and the Americans with Disabilities Act, and triumph after triumph on the international stage, even his self-sacrifice in raising taxes and righting the American economy, which was still reeling from Reagan-era deficits, all these do not erase some questionable elements in his career. He did what was necessary to win, his biographer John Meacham reminds us, because to lead one first must win. Think of the Willie Horton ad Bush allowed during his 1988 presidential campaign, making race an explicit part of our electoral politics—creating an unfortunate legacy that we struggle with today. Think about selling arms to Iran to fund illegal military adventures in Central America—a vestige of cold-war politics and hegemonic interests—and to buy back American hostages. Then pardoning those who carried out the off-the-books operations: a state acting with impunity. Surely, I imagine, there are others here thinking of this mixed legacy even as we celebrate his life and mourn his passing. I wonder how many in this hallowed space are resisting the urge to sanctify a man who himself refused to think about legacy, leaving that to others.

His unfailing civility was not lost on me when I was fortunate enough to be his guest after he lost the 1992 election to Bill Clinton. I suspect that Bush, knowing my politics diverged from his, told me a story about Chevy Chase calling him after he lost, and saying that although their politics differed, he empathized with Bush's pain and disappointment. His deft gesture not only put me at ease, it felt genuine. One day the president hosted a whale-watching expedition, taking us twenty miles out to sea. The Atlantic Ocean was so rough even the Secret Service talked of it, and many of us were seasick. Back on shore, Bush's humble, self-deprecating sense of humor appeared when someone started apologizing for our weak stomachs. He genially dismissed our concern, saying "That's nothing to be embarrassed about. I'm the fellow who threw up in the Japanese prime minister's lap."

We watch on large monitors as a caravan of black limousines pull up and the last group of dignitaries enter the sanctuary. Family members emerge from their cars and stand together while the president's casket is removed from the hearse with solemn fanfare. The bishop receives his body; we stand as the procession comes down the center aisle and the bells toll 41. My seat is on the aisle, within arm's reach. The ceremony, pomp, and circumstance are overwhelming. The president's casket rests before the altar; family take their seats. The service begins.

It is impossible to miss the contrast between the character and dignity of the departed president and that of our sitting president, seated in his pew like a schoolboy told he must attend assembly, at times with his arms folded across his chest. Brian Mulroney, who was Prime Minister of Canada when Bush was president, says: "I believe it will be said that no occupant of the Oval Office was more courageous, more principled, and more honorable than George Herbert Walker Bush" …. "When George Bush was president of the United States of America, every single head of government in the world knew that they were dealing with a gentleman, a genuine leader, one who was distinguished, resolute, and brave." I doubt few missed the irony in these words of praise.

George W. Bush says his father "Placed great value on a good joke…that's why he chose Simpson to speak." Former Senator Alan K. Simpson, a life-long friend, spoke movingly about Bush's loyalty—to friends, family, and country - and touched on Bush's grace and humility, saying "…those who travel the high road of humility in Washington DC are not bothered by heavy traffic." With avuncular intent, Simpson went on to say of Bush that "He never hated anyone. He knew what his mother and my mother always knew. Hatred corrodes the container it's carried in."

Uttered: Words of remembrance, uplifting tales, and somber reflections on the fragile beauties of democracy and peace and the Herculean efforts George H. W. Bush made to protect and foster these jewels of civilization. Day's brightening light pours through the stained-glass windows, the towering arches silently shelter a beneficence of spirit befitting the man. Celebrating his life spent in service to others, it is proper that we gather in this cathedral, whose foundations rely upon the earth which grounds it and whose grand edifice, shaken and damaged by an earthquake, reminds us of the frailty of our greatest works.

All the words, spoken; all the hymns, sung. We stand and watch the casket borne to the hearse for its last journey to Houston. The final notes sound; as they fade the sounds of the city rise again. We wait for all the dignitaries and family to depart in their motorcades, then those returning to the hotel in the buses shuffle off to their daily lives. I walk out onto the grounds and down the street, breathing crisp air, watching people who have been watching the ceremony, watching perimeters break down as the trucks leave and police open the streets to traffic. As the congestion of well-wishers, spectators, authorities, residents, commuters and all manner of travelers clears, everyone negotiates their way through this newfound freedom. There are no horns, no "Me first" boors, and, for a moment, George Herbert Walker Bush's lifelong belief that toleration is a virtue, not a vice, proves true.

Wayne Farmer
Black and White

When I was young, I saw the world
with one binary eye
in which all things were simplified
to right or wrong,
up or down,
aligned or unaligned,
ordered or di so rd er ed,
logical or emotional.

I'd roll a car window
either fully up
or fully down;
any position in-between
would make me feel uneasy
like a task left incomplete.

The same was true of lane changes.
I preferred to signal the change, and then
quickly jump to the new lane
rather than glide.

Likewise, success and failure
were absolutes, far apart.
Anything less than a total success
was a nagging failure
which demanded either a perfect fix
or a deep burial.

When my younger brother and I,
just children,
were given kits to be assembled,
just so, to make them work,
I finished mine and then I offered
to do my brother's too
not seeing that
the object of the kit was not
just to produce a working toy,
but to instruct and then reward
the student who succeeded.

Besides, I was certain that
I could do a better job;
I viewed him as unqualified
to do the task, and told myself
that it was right to save him from
the sadness that I knew he'd feel
when his attempt did not succeed.

He let me do the work
but my result did not conform
to my exacting code
that tolerated nothing less
than perfect operation.

I was crushed,
and felt enormous guilt
for having ruined his new gift
(although he really didn't care).
To fail was bad enough
but to destroy his property
was for me unpardonable,
a sign that I had overstepped
my bounds, and had,
in my enthusiasm,
damaged something valuable.

Those same feelings engulfed me
years later
when I tried to perfect the alignment
of my own toy telescope.
Instead I misaligned it;
it produced a double image
that I could not correct.
I put the toy away
and did not open it
until long years had passed;
until the pain had dulled.

Later I confessed these things
to a therapist who diagnosed my ills
and tried to help me change the way
I saw the world.
His medication helped me cope

but our discussions did not change
my attitudes about myself
and how I felt
about authority;
about responsibility.

It's not surprising that my views
determined my career. When shown
in school a demonstration of
a small machine that, on its own,
counted up in binary:
zero zero,
zero one,
one zero (it carried the one!)
one one.
I was enthralled.
Seemingly alive, it knew
how to count from one to ten
and signalled its accomplishments
with lights that accurately indicated
a zero or a one
with no grey areas in between.

If I could build machines like that
I saw that I could place my soul into
a world where everything proceeded
logically and without fault,
endlessly predictable. And if I
built it well enough
it would do its job forever
and would never fail.

But perfection was my bane

in many jobs
where getting products out the door
was more important than
making them so perfect that
they would never fail.

I worked long hours,
leaving my wife
and my child
home alone,
failing as a father while
practicing perfection that
no one really wanted.
And so my marriage failed,
breaking when in therapy
I told my wife
quite truthfully
I feared her accusations more
than I could return her love.

Today grey skies are overhead,
and grey hairs grow upon my face.
A grey fog clouds my brain
which still sees life as dangerous
and fears to take a single step
which might result in failure.

The failures of my past outweigh
the chances for a new success
that the present often brings.
"Not today", I say,
and close the door.

John Torgrimson
Revolt of the Victors

When Jean-Bertrand Aristide, the first democratically elected president of Haiti, was overthrown in 1991, thousands of Haitians fled the country by boat. Most of them ended up at the United States Naval Base in Guantanamo, Cuba, where they were given safe haven as economic refugees under President George H.W. Bush, who passed away on November 30, 2018. The Haitians were not considered political refugees. When the coup regime collapsed in 1994 under pressure from UN/US joint military forces, Aristide returned to power. Many of the boat people were repatriated to Haiti, but by 1995, a few hundred Haitians remained at the naval base, mostly unaccompanied minors and a handful of special cases on administrative-hold.

A colleague of mine from my Hong Kong days working with the United Nations High Commissioner for Refugees—UNHCR—invited me down to Cuba. The U.S. Government had invited UNHCR to recommend durable solutions on these remaining cases.

I flew down to GTMO in March 1995, Guantanamo Naval Base, "Gitmo," as it's called by local inhabitants. By then I had been working with refugees and displaced persons for more than a decade—resettlement work in Minnesota, refugee processing in the Philippines, and first asylum programming in Hong Kong. Because I had been involved in setting up Refugee Mental Health programs in the U.S. and Hong Kong, I was asked to handle any refugee mental health cases at GTMO.

The United Nations Convention related to the Status of Refugees was adopted in 1951 in response to the millions of displaced and stateless migrants in Europe following World War II. It was later broadened in the 1967 Protocol, which the United States is a signatory. The Convention/Protocol is the centerpiece of how refugees are defined today—

Owing to well-founded fear of being persecuted for reasons of race, religion, nationality, membership of a particular social group or political opinion, is outside the country of his nationality and is unable or, owing to such fear, is unwilling to avail himself of the protection of that country; or who, not having a nationality and being outside the country of his former habitual residence as a result of such events, is unable or, owing to such fear, is unwilling to return to it.

Repatriation is always the expected outcome for displaced people offered safe haven in another country. Once the conditions that led to the flight by the asylum seeker have been restored to normal, and there is no longer a fear of persecution, the foreign national is expected to return to their country of origin.

A few weeks into my consultancy, I found myself accompanying a team of UN lawyers interviewing these safe haven cases that had been placed on "administrative hold" by the U.S. Government. There were about one hundred Haitian adults, many with families, that the authorities were unsure what to do with.

What follows is a sanitized version of my official report, written nearly 25 years ago, to the UNHCR Chief of Mission in Washington, D.C. The report asserts that many of the safe haven cases being held at Guantanamo should be granted refugee status as victims of torture. It was accompanied by a list of Haitian nationals and their families.

Haitian Torture Victims
Guantanamo Naval Base
April 5, 1995

To: Chief of Mission, UNHCR
From: John Torgrimson, UNHCR-GTMO Consultant

During the period, March 23 to April 5, 1995, lawyers with UNHCR reviewed the cases of Haitians on administrative hold and afforded temporary Safe Haven Status by the US Government at Guantanamo Naval Base, Cuba. Of this group, UNHCR has determined that at least 20 cases warrant the application of refugee status under the Convention/Protocol criteria for determination of refugee status. These 20 cases will be forwarded to the State Department for consideration for refugee status and resettlement in the US.

The lawyers also believe that there may be additional cases, presently on medical hold, that may warrant refugee status. UNHCR has identified a number of cases where refugee status does not apply, but where there is "special concern" as to the future welfare of the individuals due to their documented exposure to violence and trauma.

Of these 24 cases, 12 involve the rape of female family members, often multiple times, and sometimes in front of other family members; 13 involve close family members killed, often in front of other family members; and two involve incidents of forced incestual sex.

These incidents followed in the wake of the *coup d'etat* of Aristide, and the *deshoukaj* (revolt of the victors) that followed by the Tonton Macoutes, a paramilitary group aligned with the coup government.

Approximately half of these families have been direct recipients of acts of violence or have had family members killed. There are other incidents of summary arrest, beatings, stabbings and shootings.

The motivation for these acts of persecution was the asylum seekers association with social and political organizations, and/or their relationship to a family member who was active within these organizations. The more severe cases of persecution involve people who witnessed acts of violence of family members, which was intended to coerce and/or punish the individual.

These acts of violence, may in fact, constitute "acts of torture", where severe pain or suffering (physical or psychological) are intentionally inflicted on a person for such purposes as: (a) obtaining information; (b) obtaining a confession; (c) punishment; (d) intimidation or coercion; (e) any reason based on discrimination. In addition, many of these acts were carried out by, or with the agreement of, a public official.[1]

Because of recent events in Haiti, which includes the restoration of the Aristide government and the provision of security by the US Government/United Nations forces, it could be argued that the refugee claims of the above mentioned Haitian Safe Haven cases and cases of "special concern" have ceased due to fundamental changes in country conditions.[2] Repatriation to a subject's country of origin is always the first consideration when that country's conditions cease to present the risk of persecution if the individual were to return.

However, an exception to the cessation clause recognizes that a person who has suffered under atrocious

---

[1] Acts of Torture as defined in the United Nations declaration of December 9, 1975 and the 1984 Convention Against Torture

[2] Article 1 C (5) of the 1951 Convention.

forms of persecution should never be expected to repatriate. Regardless of a change in regime, "this may not produce a complete change in the attitude of the population, nor, in view of past experiences, in the mind of the refugee."[3]

UNHCR-GTMO recommends that the US Government not repatriate those Haitians who are of "special concern" because of the severe trauma of their experiences in Haiti and urges the US Government to consider these cases for resettlement on humanitarian grounds.

The scientific literature surrounding the identification and treatment of victims of torture is very clear.

Survivors of organized violence commonly face severe psychological problems that have both short-term and long-term effects. Commonly reported feelings at the time of rape, for example, include shock, a fear of injury or death that can be paralyzing, and a sense of profound loss of control over one's life. Longer-term effects can include persistent fears, avoidance of situations that trigger memories of the violation, profound feelings of shame, difficulty remembering events, intrusive thoughts of abuse, decreased ability to respond to life generally, and difficulty re-establishing intimate relationships.

There is also a recognized cumulative effect where multiple acts of persecution and torture—"the stressors"—and the flight from persecution directly correlate to the victim's degree of trauma and psychological well-being.

In one well-documented case:

Meritane (not her real name), a woman in her early 40s, was married to a prominent businessman and Aristide supporter who was killed by Tonton Macoutes in 1993. The surviving family members witnessed the killing of Meritane's 66 year old mother and 15 year old son, the beating of her son, and the beating and rape of her daughter by four men. On the same night that her husband was killed, the military shot and killed her husband's brother in his home after discovering Aristide posters there.

Meritane's family, which now includes her two daughters and one son, spent nine months in hiding prior to fleeing Haiti. The family has been in Guantanamo since July 1994.

The long-term effects of detention, in and of itself, have been proven to be stressful to asylum seekers. People in detention show a higher incidence of anxiety, depression and other adjustment-related pathology than do populations at large. For example, recent studies of unaccompanied minors in the Hong Kong camps, whether accompanied or not, show a higher than normal incidence of acute stress-related disturbance. These symptoms were more pronounced among individuals who did not know their status and whose durable solution was delayed. Acute symptoms increased in proportion to duration in the camp. [4]

Most of the Haitian individuals identified above have lived at Guantanamo Naval Base, Cuba since July 1994. Most of them are on Safe Haven Hold, with no knowledge of what will happen to them in the future.

All of the individuals reside in Camp 7 in tents on a cement runway. There is no shade, other than the shelter of the tent. Temperatures regularly approach 90+ degrees Fahrenheit during the day - it can only be assumed that the temperature is higher in the camp itself. [5]

Under detention conditions like Guantanamo, camp residents have little or no control over their daily lives and are totally reliant on outsiders to meet their basic needs. Camp residents have little input into decision making. Even the simple act of a mother preparing food for a child cannot take place in Guantanamo.

Living conditions are very basic with approximately 10 individuals living in each tent; privacy is attempted by hanging bedding to separate family units. There are few activities for asylum seekers to engage in as daily life is regimented and institutionalized around administrative routine. Mobility is confined to the parameters of the exterior fencing. The US Government provides for the material needs of the camp residents. The camp management provides all food and the cooking of food in the camp is not allowed due to the danger of fire. Any requests for assistance (eg, to see a doctor) have to be forwarded to the military personnel administering the camp.

Detention conditions also create unintended consequences due to the institutional atmosphere of the camp. This can undermine the child/parent relationship, where the parent is no longer in control of life events. Basic parenting and nurturing roles, and the relationship between parent and child are undermined. Daily routines are dictated by camp administration and the material well-being of the individual and family is wholly dependent upon outside sources.

---

[3] Second paragraph of Article 1 C (5)

[4] Living in Detention: A Review of the Psychosocial Well-being of Vietnamese Children in the Hong Kong Detention Centers, International Catholic Child Bureau, 1992

[5] It is interesting to note that a brochure in the Bachelor's Officer Quarters in Guantanamo Naval Base advises residents not to "leave air-conditioned buildings during the months of July and August."

Given the above, it can be argued objectively that prolonged isolation in a detention setting, and in circumstances where resolution of the individual's displaced status (Safe Haven Hold) has yet to be resolved, further exacerbates the trauma, discomfort and persecution of the individual. These circumstances are anxiety producing and prolong the inability of the asylum seeker to resume a normal life and become "psychologically whole."

Recent studies conducted in Turkey on torture victims have shown that the severity of torture and its direct impact on various life areas (e.g. the family), accurately predict post-traumatic stress reactions.[6]

There is similar evidence, as found in studies conducted with Vietnam veterans suffering PTSD, that post-traumatic stress can be passed generationally from parents to children.

From these and similar studies, it has been identified that early trauma debriefing, involvement in self-help groups, assimilation into normal communities and long-term social support are effective in preventing, and/or mitigating the debilitating effects of post-traumatic stress.

Conditions in camp 7, where living conditions are basic, privacy is very limited and mobility is restricted, does not provide an adequate milieu for severe trauma victims to begin the process of healing.

Given the severe trauma experienced by the people identified in this document, it is UNHCR's recommendation that these Haitian victims of torture be allowed to resettle as soon as possible.

John Torgrimson
UNHCR Consultant
Guantanamo Bay, Cuba

Epilogue

Today there are more than 60 million displaced people in the world.

Some are economic migrants looking for a better life.

Some are seeking safe haven from the war zones in their country where it is no longer safe.

And some are fleeing persecution because of who they are due to their race, religion, association with a particular social group, or political opinion.

Meritane and her family were granted refugee status by the US Government and allowed to resettle in the United States as permanent residents.

---

[6] M. Basoglu, M. Paker, O. Paker, Psychological effects of torture: a comparison of tortured with non-tortured political activists in Turkey. American Journal of Psychiatry.

Emilio Regina

Through the Eyes of the Drunken Porter
A Comedy

List of Characters in order of appearance.
PETER: male
AGATHA: female
LADY MACBETH: female
WILLIE: male/female
MACBETH: male
FLINT: male
WITCH 1: female
WITCH 2: female
WITCH 3: female
MALCOLM: male
MACDUFF: male
BEATRICE: female
EXTRAS
SETTING: Table with chairs. A castle in Scotland. The gate is offstage and entrance for Macbeth and Lady Macbeth's soliloquies should be a different entrance than gate.
TIME: Anywhere between 1000-1600 A.D.

Lights up

PETER: *In his sleep.* Knock, knock, knock. Who's there in the name of St. Peter? I need riposte, or I'll keep thee out in the wintry chill. Who's there? *Awakes.*) Who's there? Hm, 'twas a gusty wind invading what was once a peaceful sleep. (takes a sip from his flask that is around his neck. Goes back to sleep. There is a pounding at the door) Go away! I command you vanish, you pounding demons.

AGATHA: Peter, tis I, Agatha. Come open the gate.

PETER: Go away I tell you! *More pounding at the door. Peter gets up.* Come again if this hammering be real. Methinks this pounding is a deception of my own. I'm in need of sleep. *There's more knocking.* Who's there! I command you speak or be forever cursed.

AGATHA: Tis I.

PETER: I know not a tis I.

AGATHA: Tis I, Agatha.

AGATHA: Peter!

PETER: Why Agatha, you look weatherworn and trodden.

AGATHA: You would be too. Twas a bitter travel for tender feet.

PETER: Then I needs come see you, as I am more calloused than thee.

AGATHA: Indeed, thou art in more ways than one.

PETER: And thou art blessed to condone my calloused antics. Now pray, tell me what brings you to these parts?

AGATHA: Oh, heavy day, Peter!

PETER: Pray, do tell.

AGATHA: I am without work due to a most calamitous day for all, and e'er worse for the martyrs it fell upon.

PETER: How now what terrible news! Are any familiar to me?

AGATHA: You've had acquaintance with one when she was but a babe, and a mere babe she was at the end of her shortened life. Oh Peter, Peter! She was the prettiest that e'er I nurs'd. I should live a thousand years and never forget her.

PETER: Julietta!

PETER: Agatha! Stay you there, and Peter, the not so saintly, will crack open the pearly gates for thee! *Goes off stage and opens squeaky gate.*

AGATHA: Aye, and her husband fell victim too, to the whims of their feuding families. It was the warfare between the two households that brought about their tragic end.

PETER: Oh, most lamentable day!

AGATHA: Oh, I must not think on't. It and laborious travel hath affected severe headaches and backaches so much so that I'm in need of some aqua vitae.

PETER: Ah yes, that I can, that I can. (Hands Agatha his flask of wine).

AGATHA: Why tis a goodly drink. (Agatha has changed her tone of mourning) Now, on to other business, Peter. I need occupation as nurse or what have you.

PETER: If I were king you would be my queen and I would grant you all and nurse too.

AGATHA: Tis a kind and kingly gesture but that is all.

PETER: A kind gesture is all I can tender. Lend thine ear and I shall speak of the grave state-of-affairs hither: I've overheard the thane and his lady here in King Duncan's castle scheming to dispose of him and usurp his throne. Thus, thou wouldst be better off not to serve a volatile king or the tyrant thane and his lady. If you wish to stay, I need to mask thee from these murderous tyrants. What's worse is I'm also afeard for my own position hither. *Noises off stage.* But soft, here comes the lady on her daily prattles. Tis quite the spectacle as you shall bear witness. Hide, for she breaks in and out of her mad spells. *Agatha hides.*

Enter Lady Macbeth.

AGATHA: *Peter approaches Lady Macbeth.* Stay! I beseech you. Peter come hither!

PETER: Rest your worriment, for I am sly and soundless, lest I be a fool.

AGATHA: Tis precisely the fool in you that I fear most.

PETER: Shh! She is about the speak.

LADY MACBETH: The Raven himself is hoarse
That croaks the fatal entrance of Duncan
Under my battlements. Come, you spirits
That tend on mortal thoughts, unsex me here.

PETER: Here and now, What of Macbeth? (begins to take of his shirt. *Lady Macbeth does not acknowledge Peter, as she is self-absorbed.*

AGATHA: Thou art indeed lewd! You've misconstrued her intent, you fool.

LADY MACBETH: And fill me from the crown to the toe-top full
Of direst cruelty. Make thick my blood.
Stop up the access and passage to remorse,
That no compunctious visiting of nature
Shake my fell purpose, nor keep peace between
The effect and it!

PETER: *To Agatha.* The Lady is packed with cruelty and mal-intent. *Peter is waving his hand in Lady Macbeth's face.*

LADY MACBETH: Come to my woman's breasts.

PETER: Didst thou hear her? She wants me to go to her breasts.

AGATHA: Hold, hold! Tis a booby trap if I've ever witnessed.

LADY MACBETH: And take my milk for gall.

PETER: My flask of wine will do, but I thank thee. *Takes a drink from his flask.*

LADY MACBETH: You murdering ministers,
Wherever in your sightless substances
You wait on nature's mischief. Come, thick night,
And pall thee to thy dunnest smoke of hell,
That my keen knife see not the wound it makes. *She takes out a dagger.*

PETER: Help ho, murder! *He drops to his knees and goes into a fetal position.* Agatha! Come hither chop-chop!

AGATHA: I'm on my way, Peter! *Face to face with Lady Macbeth.* Hold! Hold!

LADY MACBETH: Or heaven peep through the blanket of the dark
And cry, "Hold, Hold!"
Lady Macbeth exits with dagger in hand.

AGATHA: Well now, shall we collect ourselves, and speak of these strange happenings within the castle walls?

PETER: Aye, let us sit awhile and speak of foul deeds that are brewing hither.

Agatha: Aye, with a swig of brew to be sure. *Agatha takes Porter's flask and drinks. There is a knock at the door.*

PETER: Knock, knock, knock. Never a quiet. *Goes to the door. More pounding. Knock, knock, knock!*

WILLIE: Who's there?

PETER: Why, tis I the porter.

Willie: Wouldst thou like to enter?

PETER: What means you?

WILLIE: Upon your request I'll open the gate for thee, for tis bitter cold out there.

PETER: Why yes, tis truly cold. Thou art kind, I beseech you let the poor porter in.

AGATHA: Thou art in, fool.

PETER: Why yes, I am, indeed. You out there, I am the keeper of this hell gate and you shall not enter, lest you be made more a fool than I.

WILLIE: I am, sir, already more fool than thou art.

PETER: Very well then. That being rooted, other conditions needs be met ere entry be granted.

WILLIE: Pray tell; I've no longer the will to jest with thee, for tis bitter cold out here.

PETER: You may enter these pearly gates if one, I know thee more than mere acquaintance; two, you never play me again; and three, you regard me as king of this castle.

WILLIE: Kingly you will be treated, for tis a fool's work not to make a fool of his king unless he wants to be a headless fool. To the

other appended condition, why tis I man! Willie the fool at your service, your majesty.

AGATHA and PETER: Willie! *Peter opens gate. Enter Willie.*

AGATHA: You disguised thy voice trickily behind Peter's gate.

WILLIE: Tis a goodly craft, I do admit.

AGATHA: Your counterfeiting tomfoolery hath not lost its sharp end, e'en a wee bit.

WILLIE: Not as of yet, but when a fool hath dullened his rhetoric and muse, tis time he lay his soul and tools to rest.

AGATHA: Then forever be a witty fool and let the rest wait.

PETER: I'm with the lady on that account. Now pray do tell what draws you to these parts?

WILLIE: I'm short a king and lack shelter. Will you take poor Willie in?

PETER: Where shall I house thee? Agatha is barely accounted for.

WILLIE: Surely there must be one other crevice to tuck me in.

PETER: Should you be unearthed, we'll all be hanged. But there is temporary reprieve: so long as the tyrant and his lady have their senses dismantled we can be provisionally at ease. But you must hide from other attendants hither.

WILLIE: Consider it done and let us for now be at ease, but on other matters I am not settled in the least, for hot off the fire is a most lamentable calamity.

PETER: What means you by this?

WILLIE: Oh, the thought of it still hounds me.

AGATHA: What is't? What have you, Willie?

WILLIE: Oh, woe be mine!

AGATHA: Oh, heavy day, one more tragedy among us, and it too sounds fresh. Pray do tell if it not afflicts thee too much in thy telling.

WILLIE: Oh Agatha, Agatha! Tis too painful and too soon to e'en be coined a memory. Yet I must recount it, for when it is spoken of it quells the mind that also sees its gore.

AGATHA: Goodness! Then you need tell.

WILLIE: I'll take a wee sip first if thou shouldest so kind.

PETER: For certain. *Gives Willie his flask.*

WILLIE: The late king shouldst not have been old till he had been wise. Ere he died of a broken heart, he had given all his titles to his two vile daughters, and the third daughter, the most allegiant and trusted one, received none. By and by, the two impish ones fashioned their father in the likes of an obedient king and then banished him from his own household. And I … oh and I …

AGATHA: Go on fool, go on.

WILLIE: And I, try as I may as the king's fool, witnessed the demon daughters strip the poor

king to the point where he wished Beelzebub would take him to the better place.

PETER: Oh villainy, villainy, let the doors be locked should these two fiends make their way hither!

Willie: Fear not.

PETER: Fear not! Why I'm wet with fear! And in need of drink. *Porter drinks and passes flask to Agatha.*

WILLIE: Worry not, I say, for they did get theirs in the end: One was poisoned by the other and the other carved herself with a welcomed dagger.

AGATHA: Well they won't be coming hither anon.

WILLIE: *Pause.* Lest they come back as witches.
AGATHA and PETER: Witches!

WILLIE: Evil knows no bounds, or I be a fool.

AGATHA: *Relieved.* Well, that settles that then.

WILLIE: But say they were to come back as hags and try your gate? How wouldst thou act, Peter?

PETER: For whatever reason should they come hither?

WILLIE: Tis a strong premonition o' mine.

PETER: I will not let them in, not by the hair of my chin. I'll brave it to the end if needs be. But let a steed with better direction lead us back to our senses. I've heard gibberish talk of these weird sisters, but I've not witnessed their existence. Thus, tis a yarn conjured by some illustrious story teller.

WILLIE: I believe them to be true.

AGATHA: And I. Methinks I saw the likes of one in my travels hither, the night before last.

PETER: Balderdash! Thou wert fatigued in thy travels, and your senses were thus clouded.

Rustling within.
PETER: Didst thou hear that!

WILLIE: Tis but a wee skittish mouse.

PETER: Methinks tis was much more than that.
AGATHA: Methinks the cargo in thy flask hath been emptied a wee bit too much into thy brain.

PETER: Shh! Someone comes this way, I'm sure of't. Cloak yourselves cap a pe, chop, chop!

Enter Macbeth
MACBETH: Is this a dagger which I see before me,
The handle toward my hand? Come let me Clutch thee. *Macbeth swoops several times for the imaginary dagger. Peter approaches Macbeth.*

AGATHA: Come hither you madcap fool!

PETER: Not to worry; I've seen him in a harmless spell in the likes afore.

AGATHA: Do you see a dagger afloat?

PETER: No.

WILLIE: Nor do I.

AGATHA: His faculties have deserted him.

Peter follows Macbeth around.
MACBETH: I have thee not, and yet I see thee still.
Art thou not, a fatal vision sensible
To the feeling as to sight?

The others curiously trail behind Peter, who is behind Macbeth.
PETER: Methinks I see it!

Agatha: Tis a phantom dagger, fool.

PETER: I confess twas a mere speckle in mine eye.

MACBETH: Or art thou but
A dagger of the mind, a false creation,
Proceeding from the heat-oppressed brain?

WILLIE: He's a castle short of a few towers, thus tis likely as he claims.

MACBETH: I see thee yet, in the form as palpable
As this which now I draw. *Draws a dagger.*

PETER: Help ho murder! Is that a dagger? Or is't a fabrication of a pickled brain? I know not. Help ho!

AGATHA: Tis a true one! Brace thyself, Peter!

Porter curls up into a fetal position.
Peter: Help ho!

MACBETH: Thou marshall'st me the way that I was going:
And such an instrument I was to use.

Mine eyes are made the fools o' the other senses.

WILLIE: Tis a confirmation of his own madness.

MACBETH: I see thee still.

PETER: He sees me still, help ho!

AGATHA: Tis reference to the phantom dagger, fool.

Macbeth turns away from Peter. They follow Macbeth aimlessly around. A bell chimes several times. They all shutter.
PETER: Oh, what an eerie sounding knell!

MACBETH: I go, and it is done: the bell invites me.
Hear it not, Duncan, for it is a knell
That summons thee to heaven or to hell.
Exit Macbeth.

PETER: He's off to murder the king.

WILLIE: Indeed. He hath madly voiced it, and we the witnesses have heard.

Knock on the door. They all freeze.
PETER: Is this a knock I hear or has my ear been made the fool o' the other senses?

More knocking.
PETER: Methinks tis a knocking upon my heat intoxicated brain and I'll be the fool who opens gates to greet the wind.

AGATHA: Tis a knocking at thy gate, fool.

PETER: Art thou sure?

AGATHA: As sure as thou hast fodder for brains. Now go to as a keeper shouldst and we'll conceal ourselves.

PETER: Who's there?

FLINT: A pauper or clown whichever you wish to adopt.

PETER: We have abundance of clowns and paupers hither; we need not an extra.

FLINT: I am otherwise the chert in chalk, and creator of spark.

ALL: Flint!

PETER: That be you, Flint?

FLINT: I am he.

PETER: Come in, come in.

FLINT: Greetings Peter, Willie, Agatha.

PETER: What do we owe the pleasure, pray?

AGATHA: That I can surely answer. You are out of work.

FLINT: No, tis too much work, I fear.

WILLIE: How now, what means you?

FLINT: Oh, woe is me.

AGATHA: Oh, dear!

FLINT: Oh, heavy day. Too much blood for one day.

AGATHA: Not another! We are in desperate need of comedy. I pray you enlighten us first, Flint.

FLINT: If Flint could he would flicker a light in thee, but tis too damp a day to kindle a spark.

AGATHA: Oh, woe upon woe; It doesn't get any darker than midnight, and now this. E'en as it pains us, I ask that you do tell, for we are here to sooth thee.

FLINT: Oh, I shall speak as one with tired spade in hand. When sorrows come, they come not as single spies but in battalions.

AGATHA: Oh, tis too much to bare! And you've yet to note the items you speak of.

FLINT: Aye, now brace yourselves, for I will not draw it out and tell it all in one breath: The wretched King, his queen, the mad prince, his princess to be, her father and scores more murdered, murdered!

WILLIE: Oh, my, there is no room at all for play here.

FLINT: This is the least of all the tragedies.

AGATHA: Oh, I don't think I could bare it, please no more.

WILLIE: Go on Flint.

FLINT: And I, oh and I …

WILLIE: Have courage Flint.

FLINT: And I with spade in hand was assigned as their gravedigger.

WILLIE: Why tis so many graves to dig for one digger.

FLINT: So much digging didst I to the point where I exhumed the bones o' their forefathers. Oh horrid, horrid. And even more horrid, on that day, my spade hit a skull recognizable.

WILLIE: Whose skull, dare I ask?

FLINT: Tis Yorick's, the King's jester.

WILLIE: Oh, my. I knew him well. A fellow of infinite jest, of most excellent fancy. He hath borne me on his back a thousand times and taught me his trade. Poor Yorick.

FLINT: He drunk himself to death, the poor fellow did. I need to pause for a stoup of liquor. *He takes out his own flask of liquor and a skull from a sack. They all gasp.*

AGATHA: What a ghastly sight!

PETER: He looks quite chapfallen.

WILLIE: Whose skull is it?

FLINT: Why tis Yorick's.

WILLIE: Tis not a digger's code to be taking someone's skull. You bring severe punishment upon thyself.

FLINT: Tis reason for it.

WILLIE: Pray, do tell if thou wish to uphold thy name.

FLINT: Yorick's skull hath special powers to ward off evil spirits. Tis proven when you hold the skull thus … *He demonstrates* … it fends off spirits, hags, ghosts, and even wolves if you tip it thus and howl.

WILLIE: Where did you learn this?

FLINT: Why from Yorick.

WILLIE: I must say tis a hard thing to believe in spirits, witches and ghosts. Tis all fibs, I say.

FLINT: I believe them to be true. Methinks I saw three warty hags in my travels hither.

AGATHA: And I. Why p'raps the same ones. How were the looks o' them?

FLINT: I know not. They were quick to vanish as soon as I lay eyes on them. But I know of their hideous laughter and foul smell, for that is what lingered in the eerie air.

Wolves howling.
PETER: Oh, what frightful cries. Give me that skull. *Takes skull from Flint and holds it upside down and howls.*

FLINT: Tis not the proper formality. The keeper of the skull is the only one who shall use it, unless thy wish is to be turned into stone.

Peter yelps and throws skull back to Flint. There is loud thunder. Some rustling from off stage.
Peter: Who goes there? *To the others.* Hide, lest ye be made into mince!

Enter Lady Macbeth
LADY MACBETH: Out damn spot! Out, I say! Who would have
Thought the man to have had so much blood in him?

PETER: Do you mark that? She alludes to the king. Methinks both powermongers have slaughtered the king. Oh, heavy day. I'm now a porter without a gate. Tis a new order now with a new crew. I'll porter it no more. Oh, woe is mine! *Peter approaches Lady Macbeth.*

WILLIE: Will you come hither; we'll all be hanged on your behalf!

PETER: Need not to worry. She is in the same spell as afore. She is here, yet she is not.

LADY MACBETH: Here's the smell of blood still: all the
Perfumes of Arabia will not sweeten this little hand. Oh! Oh!
Oh!

PETER: Do you smell blood?

AGATHA: No.

PETER: Nor I.

LADY MACBETH: Wash your hands, put on your night-gown.

PETER: Yes, tis a grand idea. Now be off with you.

There's pounding at the gate.
LADY MACBETH: To bed, to bed: there's knocking at the gate.

PETER: Shall I trust the madcap? Is't that knocking true?

There's pounding at the door.
AGATHA: It is not.

PETER: Methought as much.

LADY MACBETH: Come, come, come, come, give me your hand: what's done,
Cannot be undone: to bed, to bed, to bed.

PETER: Yes, to bed. *Peter gives Lady Macbeth his hand.*

AGATHA: Will you let go of her hand, fool and go see who awaits thee at thy pearly gate!

PETER: Didst thou not say there is no knocking?

AGATHA: That I did say.

PETER: Then I'm befuddled.

AGATHA: Tis a common state of yours. Now will you go see who's pounding upon your portal. Tis not a knocking in the least. Now go to! And we'll cloak ourselves.

PETER: Who's there?

WITCH 1: The sisters three with stew.

PETER: Stew who?

WITCH 1: Tis brew, if that be a better word than stew.

Peter: Brew who? Declare thyself i' the name of Beelzebub.

WITCH 1: Tis the weird sisters three.

FLINT: By the pricking of my thumb, methinks something wicked this way comes.

PETER: Who's there in the other devil's name?

WITCH 1: Tis the weird sisters three. Now open this confounded hell-gate or I'll conjure a great wind to squeeze us through a chink 'tween floor and gate.

Peter: 'twood be a sorcerer's trick indeed. And that you are not, for I've seen none in me life. *Pounding.* Knock, knock. Never at quiet! What are you!

WITCH 1: Tis thrice and one we have informed thee. And now without ado or customary politeness we'll deflate, compress, and wedge through an infinitesimal slit upon thy gate.

PETER: Then summon up a windy wind and come through the chink as you profess. I'll hell porter it no more. I'm in the spirit for some devilry. P'raps a swig of wine will aid me with what you allege. *Takes a drink from a flask he has around his chest.* Go to, I will bare witness to your preposterous scheme. Come on!

Enter Witch 1,2,3. Witch 2 has a drum she taps for effect, Witch 3 has some brew in a cup.

PETER: Hello! Why tis unthinkable. What are you?

WITCH1: We are the weird sisters three.

AGATHA: It's them! The ones I saw yesternight!

FLINT and WILLIE: And I.

FLINT: Oh, a most hideous sight!

AGATHA: Unveil Yorick and spell drift them to some foreign place.

FLINT: Aye and forthwith. (Takes out Yorick's skull. Witches cower) This skull I raise before thee and command you take your leave else turn to musty dust in the catacombs of Ninny's Tomb.

AGATHA: Methinks tis Ninus' Tomb.

FLINT: Tis what I meant.

WITCH 1: Put that away, I command you!

FLINT: I will not, you filthy hags. You'll not get me.

WITCH 2: We have concocted means to counteract the spell o' skulls.

FLINT: Tis not a mere common skull. Tis Yorick's.

ALL WITCHES: Yorick's!

FLINT: Aye, indeed.

WILLIE: Mark their horror and dismay. We have them affright, Flint! Tis a worthy skull to lug around.

FLINT: What are they plotting? Away I say, you feculent, repulsive hags.

Witch 2 takes out a book and flips through it frantically. Witches begin to circle around Flint and chant the verses with accompanied drum. Verses could also be chanted by all witches.
WITCH 2: If this be the skull o' thee historic Yorick,
Transform it we shall as other skulls generic
And take thy power away from thy boney jaw
By the circular waving of a monkey's paw,
Witch 3 waves a monkey's paw around the skull.

By the meowing and hissing of we Witches three *Witches hiss and meow.*
Till the keeper buckles upon his left knee
And cries "Hold!"

FLINT: *Desperately.* Hold!

WITCH 2: And surrenders the boney skull …
Flint gives skull to Witch 1.
To be bagged, tightly sealed and render null.
Witch 3 puts skull back into Flint's bag.

WITCH 1: Now back to our business.

PETER: I beseech you, what is thy purpose hither?

WITCH 2: To prophesy with a regal swine.

PETER: *Relieved.* Ah, you want Macbeth. Hold up, and I'll call him hither.

WITCH 3: The hurly burly hath been done with Macbeth.

PETER: If not Macbeth, then with whom?
Witch 2 starts beating drum. Peter is not sure what to do, as witches approach him. Witch 2 taps a rhythm on drum.

AGATHA: Methinks you're the one they've in mind.

WILLIE: Oh, poor Peter, porter and swine!

PETER: Why surely, ye jest. It cannot be. I'm a lowly drunken porter.

Drum beats harder. Peter starts to do a jig to the rhythm of the drum.

WITCH 1: Halt! *Peter freezes.* Do not mock our business hither. We have come to acquaint thee with forthcoming events bound to thy destiny.

PETER: I've not the ambition to be acquainted with it; now shrivel thee further into tiny hags, and slip through the crevice from whence ye came, or gentleman I'll be and draw the gate for thee.

Peter goes to exit but is blocked by the Witches. Witch 2 gets a stool and places it around CS.

PETER: Ah, a stool. tis what I crafted. Carpentry is my most favored occupation and then drinking. No, drinking is my …

WITCH 2: Sit.

PETER: Sit?

WITCH 1,2,3: SIT!

AGATHA, FLINT, WILLIE: SIT!

Witch 3 hands Peter the cup with potion in it.

PETER: No thank you. A kind gesture, but I'm a little swollen e'en for a wee nip.

WITCH 3: Drink.

PETER: Drink?

WITCH 1,2,3: Drink!

AGATHA, WILLE, FLINT: Drink!

Peter drinks.

PETER: Mm, tis a goodly brew. What's in't?

WITCH 3: Eye of toad, fillet of snake, eye of newt, toe of frog, wool of bat, tong of dog,

adder's folk, lizard's leg, scale of dragon, and tooth of wolf.

Porter gags for each ingredient spoken. For the last ingredient he sticks fingers in mouth. Witch 1 pulls his fingers out of his mouth.

WITCH 1: Hold, hold, hold!

Witch 2 begins to beat drum rhythmically. Porter pulls out his flask and takes a drink to kill the taste of the witches' brew. Witch 1,2,3 start circling around Peter. There is thunder.

WITCH 1: All hail the porter!

WITCH 1,2,3: Hail to the porter! *Witch 1 looks vehemently to Willie, Flint, and Peter.*

WILLIE: Are we to teem with thee in thy Ritual?

WITCH 1: ALL hail the porter!

ALL: Hail to the porter!

PETER: I thank thee. Tis a most grand ceremony, I must say.

WITCH1: All hail the porter who shall continue to be the keeper of the gate if it be his preference.

PETER: If the choice is to be or not to be a porter, I shall prefer to take the first.

WITCH 1: The second hath not yet been revealed.

PETER: I wish not to know the other; I fear it does not bode so well.

WITCH 1: Be it so. The first shall suffice for now.

PETER: I thank thee, and wish no further conference, lest it be for the others, then lay on and look into the seeds of time and say which grain will grow and which will not.

WITCH 1: Speak.

WITCH 2: Demand.

WITCH 3: We'll answer.

FLINT: Do not let them pry further, or yours will be a tragic end.

PETER: Tis not for me.

FLINT: For whom?

PETER: You need yours told as well.

AGATHA: Do not dare conjoin us in thy prophecy, Peter!

PETER: Tis all good, or else I'm not keeper of the gate. Now allow me to do further business with the good sisters. *To the witches.* I thank thee to keep me as keeper of the gate as for now, but what shall become of my wretched allies? *He refers to Willie, Agatha and Flint.*

WILLIE: We shall have prophecy as well.

FLINT: Twill not be a favorable forecast.

AGATHA: I fear it also.

WITCH 3: Upon further drink from the porter, we shall reveal.

PETER: I'll pass, thank you.

WITCH 1,2,3: Drink!

AGATHA, WILLIE, FLINT: Do not drink!
Peter gulps from cup. Witches are behind Peter who is still on stool. Witches look up. Thunder.

WITCH 1: Give me wind.

WITCH 2: I'll give thee wind.

WITCH 1: Thou art kind.

WITCH 3: And I another.

WITCH 1: I myself have all the other.

PETER: Tis a rank and foul wind. *Peter gags.*

WITCH 3: Hold thy tongue and prick thine ear.

WITCH 1: The prophetic winds of time hath given augur to theirs. *Points to Flint, Agatha, Willie.*

WILLIE: We do not want ours revealed.

WITCH 1: Then so be it.

WILLIE: I thank thee, kind sisters.

WITCH 1: The other choice is sudden death.

FLINT: Then give us the first ye foul beldams!

WITCH 1: Each fate hinges upon the Porter's choice of position and status.

PETER: Let it be so then. I still choose to be porter, and the other I will decline, for tis a trap. My mates and I shall manage, e'en under the rule of the tyrannous Macbeth if it be so. *He takes a drink from his flask.* Now take thy foul brew and repulsive air and exit from whence you came. Too much exposition in thy telling hath given way to a pounding in my head.

WITCH 1: We shall not leave till all is revealed.

WITCH 1: Give me wind

WITCH 2: I'll give thee wind.

WITCH 1: Thou art kind.

WITCH 3: And I another.

WITCH 1: I myself have all the other.

Flint, Willie, Agatha and Peter gag.
PETER: Must you give wind for every foretelling? *There is thunder.*

WITCH 1: Hush, as the winds o' destiny give way to vision and verse.

WITCH 2: I see it now.

WITCH 1: Then tell it.

WITCH 2: A battle one-on-one shall be fought and won
By tyrant and thane in the midnight sun.
Let the porter's gate be freely unlatched
And let the two mysteries be unhatched.

Enter Macbeth and Macduff. They battle with swords.
MACBETH: I'll not fight thee.

MACDUFF: Then yield thee, coward,
And live to be the show and gaze o'th' time.

We'll have thee, as our rarer monsters are,
Painted upon a pole, and underwrit,
'Here may you see the tyrant'.

PETER: Why tis Macbeth and Macduff. They battle: One for monarchy, the other revenge.

MACBETH: I will not yield,
To kiss the ground before young Malcolm's feet,
And to be baited with a rabble's curse.
lay on Macduff, and damned be him that first
Cries 'Hold, enough'.
Exit Macbeth and Macduff.

WILLIE: What means this?

PETER: That I can answer: If the tyrant lives he shall still be king, and you'll all be hanged.

WILLIE, AGATHA, FLINT: *Ad lib.* Oh, woe is mine! It cannot be!

PETER: The better outcome wouldst be if Macbeth is mortally wounded, then the late king's first son Malcolm will be crowned. Let us hope the latter and you'll all be spared.

AGATHA, FLINT, WILLIE: Let us hope for the latter. Indeed! Oh, let that be the one!

WITCH 1: Well done! Thou hath scrupulously expounded on the conceivable consequences, but the final outcome yet to be disclosed shall reveal all and nullify your forecasts. Lest ye forget, we witches three are the masters of oracle.

PETER: Well, then stop playing us and get on with it!

WITCH 1: 'Hanging' is an operative word in thy present matters, for a brutal outcome in the likes of a hanging will present itself anon.

PETER: Oh, woe be mine! Tis my brutal and tragic outcome they speak of to be sure!
Sounding of a bell.

AGATHA: I forewarned you of any further dealings with the weird sisters. Now the bell tolls for thee, Peter.

PETER: No! I beg of you!

WITCH 1: Silence … Give me wind.

PETER: Oh, horrid still. Spare me thy wind and hang me the sooner.

WITCH 2: I'll give thee wind.

WITCH 1: Thou art kind.

WITCH 3: And I another.

WITCH 1: I myself have all the other.

WITCH 2: Of the three to enter, one will not yap,
 Two come whole, other a mere cap.
As future king goes about his lofty speech
And conveys to ye of a tyrant's breach,
A tragic twist will unfold in this very room,
That will put one more beside the late king's tomb,
And make way to a jocose sequel for some
But for a one a most lamentable one.

PETER: Swear ye shall lament upon my tragic end.

AGATHA: I swear.

FLINT: And I.

WILLIE: And I too.
Enter Macduff and Malcolm. Macduff has Macbeth's head.

PETER: Look on't! Macduff has had his revenge upon Macbeth and Malcolm shall be king!

MACDUFF: Hail, king! For so thou art. Behold where stands
Th'userper's cursed head: the time is free:
I see thee compassed with thy kingdom's pearl,
That speak my salutation in their minds;
Whose voice I desire aloud with mine:
Hail, king of Scotland!

ALL: Hail, king of Scotland!

MALCOLM: We shall not spend a large expense of time
Before we reckon with your several loves,
And make us even with you. My thanes and kinsmen,
Henceforth be earls, the first that ever Scotland
In such an honour named.
So, thanks to all at once, and to each one,
Whom we invite to see us crowned at scone.
Malcolm drops to his knees. Peter goes to Malcolm.

PETER: Look to the king. Oh, villainy!

MALCOLM: I am dead Macduff.

MACDUFF: How can it can be? We fought as one side by side,

Our backs to one another through mud and mire.

MALCOLM: The tyrant hath given a fatal blow
Ere he was lanced and promptly beheaded.

PETER: Oh, our future king!

MALCOLM: Macduff, report me and my case aright.

MACDUFF: I shall report all and be loyal to
Whatever request you have ere you pass.

PETER: Oh, what a loss! Oh, heavy day!

MALCOLM: You sirrah, who shows so much compassion
Yours is genuine for a dying king.

PETER: Oh, your majesty, what's to be done?

MALCOLM: *To Peter.* I shall burden thee to be the next king.
Your display of love for a dying king
Is full proof that thou hath the choice making
Of a goodly king for all of Scotland.
See to't Macduff that he is crowned at scone,
And all ye bear witness to what hath been
Spoken this day for our country Scotland.
Malcolm dies

ALL: Hail, king of Scotland! *Flint takes out a crown from his sack and places it on Peter's head. All cheer.*

AGATHA: Oh, Peter, thou art in need of a queen.

PETER: To be sure of it, my love.

AGATHA: Thou art a proper, regal fool. All hail the king of Scotland!

ALL: Hail, king of Scotland!

FLINT: A speech is in order.

ALL: Speech, speech …

Peter motions all to quiet down. All are silenced and just as Peter is about to speak, there is knocking at the gate. All gasp and are uneasy.
PETER: Who comes here? Speak.

BEATRICE : Tis Beatrice. E*nter Beatrice.*

ALL: Beatrice! *Ad lib greetings from all.*

BEATRICE: Why such a festive ambiance hither?

PETER: Tis much ado about nothing.

AGATHA: Tis a portly jest, for there is much ado hither, Beatrice.

BEATRICE: Pray, do tell.

AGATHA: Peter is to be crowned at scone!

BEATRICE: Oh, let us carouse the occasion. There are scores more at thy gate, your majesty; shall I grant them entrance?

PETER: Let no soul be left out in the cold; all are welcomed in my house!

FLINT: Here, here!

Cheering and ad lib from all. It's up to the director to determine how many extras enter and how they may reflect some of Shakespeare's comic characters that are found in his plays.

PETER: *Motions crowd to quiet down.* We shall not spend a large expense of time:

All ye present shall henceforth be earls, thanes, (there are cheers)
For I will be a goodly king to thee
So, thanks to all at once, and to each one,
Whom we invite to see us crowned at scone.
More cheering.
End

Tom Driscoll
Everybody has one
Desertification

This memorably wintery winter issue of *Folk Opera* is dedicated to the lifetimes of four rural literary champions—Scott Dixon, Pixie Youngdahl, Donna Halvorson and Dean Harrington.

Scott, who lost his battle with cancer just before Christmas 2018, was a playwright, actor and director. For many years, Scott entertained audiences at the Commonweal Theater in Lanesboro, Minnesota.

Pixie Youngdahl, a retired RN, former hospice nurse, and author of the novel *Timeless Café,* wrote a cancer-survivor memoir, *Arguments & Negotiations,* published by Shipwreckt Books in 2013. A long-time member of the Minneapolis Writers Workshop, Pixie brought the spirit of collaborative criticism and production with her when she retired to rural Peterson, Minnesota in 2007. After nearly five years of remission, Pixie's cancer returned and took her in August 2018.

Donna Halvorson, a prolific poet and storyteller, the author of several books and an energetic member of writing groups, spent her life on the Upper Mississippi. Donna worked as a real estate agent and business owner. She survived her first heart attack and learned to live with heart failure decades before she passed away in January 2019 at the age of 91. To the very end of her life, Donna remained an active writer.

Dean Harrington also passed in January. Dean grew up on a farm, became a bank president and a dedicated and creative advocate for economic development in his community, including rural arts. Dean, in fact, cultivated a literary garden in Plainview, Minnesota—the Jon Hassler Theater and gallery, the Rural America Writers' Center, the *Green Blade* literary journal, and the Common Sense bookstore—a unique, small-in-scale cultural ecosystem on the prairie just northeast of Rochester, the home of Mayo Clinic and its high-powered Destination Medical Center economic development initiative.

Dean not only articulated a vision of literary culture—that is to say, incubating and sustaining writers and writing—with the RAWC, but he devoted many years to implementing a rural, arts-based economic alternative to commercial franchises: the Rural America Arts Partnership. Indeed, the now defunct Jon Hassler Theater focused on performance art, like theaters in nearby towns: the fabulously successful Commonweal Theater company and the Great River Shakespeare Festival in Winona. But Dean went further than performance; he cleared ground for wordsmiths, storytellers, poets and creative writers of every stripe to practice their art in a collaborative environment.

What these four people had in common, besides the calm fearlessness they displayed at the end, is that they devoted much of their creative life to clearing and holding the ground of literary culture. Dean's absence in particular marks the loss of a literary oasis—the broader term I use is desertification.

There are no shortage of non-profit arts organizations. Theater, music and gallery spaces flourish thanks in no small part to philanthropists and supporters who love to dress up and attend a good show. Sure, there remain many writers' groups and open mics, opportunities for writers to share time with like-minded others. But the cultural infrastructure for sowing and cross-pollinating what it is that writers do is slowly disappearing. When most writers put down their notebooks and step away from their keyboards to share ideas and criticisms, try out untested forms and publicly push the literary envelope with a new, unpublished work, they find themselves not in a *salon*, but in a cultural desert. The act of writing is arguably a performance art—but it's no stretch to say that most writers practice their craft privately as a form of disciplined creative meditation, which means that watching most writers write is like watching paint dry.

University lit and creative writing programs represent a distinct cultural sector, but the universities are guarded and proprietary about their workshops. When I refer to the literary cultural desert, I envision local university writing programs inside a bubble, a sealed terrarium, water and nutrient rich, untouched by the general desertification that surrounds them.

As a literary publisher with a clear regional interest, witnessing the closure of the Rural America Writers' Center in Plainview, and termination of the Winona Poet Laureate position in favor of an Arts Ambassador post is alarming. Performance and gallery art sectors thrive; libraries and their advocates assert unyielding allegiance to *The Book* though independent bookstores, those that remain in the wake of the Amazon tsunami, struggle for every nickel; and the literary sector—that damned place in writers' imagination that is articulated in word and image and metaphor with or without books sandwiched between covers as we've come to know them—languishes as desertification encroaches. The region of southeast Minnesota, northern Iowa and west central Wisconsin that many Shipwreckt authors and poets call home, where their inspiration resides, needs new champions, more cultural trailblazers to break a path and clear ground where writers of every skill level can sow their wildest ideas, crosspollinate, learn to receive helpful criticism, and practice and practice and improve their craft.

Advances in software, the internet and the business of self-publishing allow practically anyone to try their hand at writing. Writers are not disappearing, they're coming out of the woodwork. This phenomenon correlates at least empirically to the steady growth in the number of submissions that come over the online transom to Shipwreckt Books and *Lost Lake Folk Opera* magazine—many, I must add, of frustratingly poor quality.

Writers have been slow to adapt to the inescapable performance standard required by the arts-grant-grantors to emerging and established writers. Consumers of writing today, self-described book lovers, rightly expect more than just another skinny chapbook or an obligatory book signing by an unknown author. They want a performance too. The most popular writers today—and I'm talking about the second and third tier group of authors who can't afford to quit their day jobs—are comfortable and entertaining on stage, as well as being good writers on the page.

Traditional poetry and story readings, and open mics with time limits, place a writer at a lectern or podium before a usually small, hushed crowd—a high-priest at an altar before a mesmerized congregation. The trope is tiresome. The fact is, good writing when it's read is often boring; and bad writing goes unchallenged. They both get polite applauds. It's too often an empty oral ritual in homage to an ancient deity with frayed ties to today's evolving traditions. Sure, there are good readers, good entertainers; but good writers who lack stage presence turn invisible and mute in the literary cathedral. Spoken word and slam poetry have challenged and disrupted the traditional literary-reading paradigm largely for the better. But by dismissing the bedrock literary canon, these hybrid written/performed forms perch on shallow foundation just as susceptible to desertification as the traditional modes they displace.

Three things need to happen here south of the vibrant Twin Cities' literary scene—north of Iowa City and west of Madison—to reclaim cultural territory for a literary incubator that produces (or should produce) material for publishing and performance writing arts.

1. Creative development infrastructure outside of the university writing degree programs—critical writing workshops that emphasize improvement over self-indulgence, with outcomes that the grantors call *Capstone Events*: publication in magazines and books, production of plays, operas. Literary culture needs more private philanthropic investment and strong, sustainable for- & non-profit, strictly literary, umbrella organizations.

2. Collaboration and crosspollination incubators—coffeehouses, taverns & cafes, bookstores & libraries, co-working artist spaces and studios; these and other venues provide a nurturing environment for writers who want to explore new performance forms while continuing to grow and improve as language artists.

3. It should go without saying, but it must be said: a vibrant literary culture in the second decade of the 21st century requires great diversity, diversity of every ethno-cultural aspect—race, gender, sexual-orientation, age, literary tradition, religion, geography, language; you name it. So let's do it. As one generation of champions gracefully withdraws from the scene, the next and the next and the next forces of nature, writers, editors, mentors, organizers and donors need to irrigate and cultivate the soil of literary culture before it becomes lost to desertification.

315 S. Broadway Rochester, Minnesota

Shipwreckt Books at the Twin City Book Fair October 2018

www.ingramcontent.com/pod-product-compliance
Lightning Source LLC
Chambersburg PA
CBHW082050220626
47052CB00006B/1201